More Sex Talk

More Sex Talk

A New Collection of Ribald, Raunchy, and Provocative Quotations

Edited by James Wolfe

CITADEL PRESS
Kensington Publishing Corp.
www.kensingtonbooks.com

CITADEL PRESS BOOKS are published by

Kensington Publishing Corp.
850 Third Avenue
New York, NY 10022

Copyright © 2002 James Wolfe

All Kensington titles, imprints, and distributed lines are available at special quantity discounts for bulk purchases for sales promotions, premiums, fund-raising, educational, or institutional use. Special book excerpts or customized printings can also be created to fit specific needs. For details, write or phone the office of the Kensington special sales manager: Kensington Publishing Corp., 850 Third Avenue, New York, NY 10022, attn: Special Sales Department, phone 1-800-221-2647.

CITADEL PRESS and the Citadel logo are Reg. U.S. Pat. & TM Off.

First printing: December 2002

10 9 8 7 6 5 4 3 2 1

Printed in the United States of America

Library of Congress Control Number: 2002110881

ISBN: 0-8065-2418-9

Contents

Contents

Preface

MORE SEX TALK. That was the demand from readers
of my previous collection, *Sex Talk*. And that is
what these pages deliver. Just like the original, this
book concentrates exclusively on the subject everyone
finds most interesting.

More than 1400 new raunchy, controversial, thought-
provoking, outrageous, humorous, and thoroughly
entertaining statements by rock, movie, and sports celeb-
rities, politicians and statesmen, royalty, generals, writ-
ers, philosophers, scientists, scholars, and other notables
will be found here. Over 850 quote authors share their
most intimate insights, confessions, gossip, opinions
about all things sexual; fantasies, preferences, love and
marriage, adultery, orgasms, seduction and sixty other
categories. You name it, some notable has something to
say about it, some pundit has sage advice to offer.

The major criteria for selection was the entertain-
ment value of the quote. Is it scandalous? Profound?
Was it said by someone with gravitas or special exper-
tise? Is it provocative? Controversial? Funny? Does it
add to the continuous debate between the sexes?

Although no claims are made with respect to social
or educational value, a high-school teacher in Ohio
used the original *Sex Talk* in a sex education course because the book helped open and expand classroom dis-
cussions. Each new subject was introduced by reading

the quotations in the appropriate category, relaxing the students and fostering a more purposeful discussion. The quotes were collected from hundreds of sources. Books, magazines, radio, television, and the internet were scrutinized for suitable items. All quotes were obtained from previously published or broadcast sources and are assumed to be accurate. Considerable effort went into checking each one, but no warranty of the accuracy of all the sources is offered. The quotes are, of course, the opinions of those who first wrote or spoke them.

If you have heard or read something worthwhile that might be included in a future edition or sequel of this book, please forward it to me c/o Citadel Press/Kensington Publishing Corp. Please include the source with each quotation.

Thanks and have fun!

More Sex Talk

Advice

Do not insult a woman before she has undressed.

—African proverb

Remember, if you smoke after sex, you're doing it too fast.

—Woody Allen

Nothing is so much to be shunned as sex relations.

—St. Augustine

Here's a rule I recommend. Never practice two vices at once.

—Tallulah Bankhead

Eats first, morals after.

—Bertolt Brecht

Dump a tray of ice in your wash basin and splash ice water on your bazooms. It keeps them firm.

—Joan Crawford offering a
beauty tip to a female reporter

It's OK to laugh in the bedroom as long as you don't point.

—Will Durst

I wouldn't recommend a sauna before lovemaking.

—Britt Ekland

Don't drink water; fish fuck in it.

—W. C. Fields

Every man should be fucked up the arse as a prelude to fucking a woman, so he'll know what it's like to be the receiver. Otherwise, he'll think he's doling out joy unlimited to every woman he fucks.

—Germaine Greer

Though you love your wife, do not tell her all you know; tell her some trifle, and conceal the rest.

—Homer

Sex is hardly ever just about sex.

—Shirley MacLaine

Be strong, believe in freedom and in God, love yourself, understand your sexuality, have a sense of humor, masturbate, don't judge people by their religion, color, or sexual habits, love life and your family.

—Madonna

When things don't work well in the bedroom, they don't work well in the living room either.

—William Masters

If a man comes to your front door saying he is conducting a survey and asks you to show him your boobs, do not show him your boobs! This is a scam, and he is only trying to see your boobs.

—*Newsweek* magazine on e-mail warnings

Stay away from girls who cry or who look like they get pregnant easily or have careers.

—P. J. O'Rourke

My advice is to keep two mistresses. Few men have the stamina for more.

—Ovid

Never go to bed with anyone whose emotional problems are greater than your own.

—Satchel Paige

Never run after a bus or a man—there'll be another one along in a minute.

—Dorothy Parker

Sex is never an emergency.

—Elaine Pierson

Never floss a stranger.

—Joan Rivers

There's very little advice in men's magazines, because men think, "I know what I'm doing. Just show me somebody naked."

—Jerry Seinfeld

Put 200 condoms in a box someplace in the house where everybody isn't all the time, so that your kids can take them.

—Sharon Stone

If you want something said, ask a man. If you want something done, ask a woman.

—Margaret Thatcher

Put off your shame with your clothes when you go to your husband and put it on again when you come out.

—Theano

A wife's advice is not worth much, but woe is the husband who refuses to take it.

—Welsh proverb

A man can be a great lover, but no matter how well he performs, sex won't compensate for personality, intelligence, consideration, and whatever else you may be looking for. You may think you're in love when the passions of sex get hold of you, but if you didn't love the man before, you won't love him after. Like him, maybe— but not love him.

—Mae West

Some tickling or telling funny stories in bed can make sex more interesting.

—Dr. Ruth Westheimer

Aging

I refuse to admit that I'm more than fifty-two even if that does make my sons illegitimate.

—Lady Nancy Astor

At age eighty-two, I sometimes feel like a twenty-year-old, but there is seldom one around.

—Milton Berle

You'll have to ask somebody older than me.

—Eubie Blake, ninety, when asked at what age the sex drive ends

I'm trying to understand this generation. They have adjusted the time table for childbearing so that menopause and teaching a sixteen-year-old how to drive will occur the same week.

—Erma Bombeck

Sex can be fun after eighty, after ninety, and after lunch.

—George Burns

I can remember when the air was clean and the sex was dirty.

—George Burns

I'm at the in-between age. I still want sex very badly, I just want it before 10 p.m.

—Kim Castle

Men make love more intensely at twenty but make love better, however, at thirty.

—Catherine II, Russian empress

Setting a good example for your children takes all the fun out of middle age.

—William Feather

As you get older the pickings get slimmer but the people don't.

—Carrie Fisher

Being a sixty-four-year-old sex symbol is a hell of a weight to carry.

—John Forsythe on fame later in life

The truth is that women aren't interesting before thirty. Men are kind of born people.

—Jodie Foster

Quite a few women told me, one way or another, that they thought it was sex, not youth, that's wasted on the young.

—Janet Harris

Sensuality reconciles us with the human race. The misanthropy of the old is due in large part to the fading of the magic glow of desire.

—Eric Hoffer

A lot of people start to fall to bits at thirty . . . Once you are able to reproduce you're over the hill. You start to go downhill at eighteen physically.

—Mick Jagger

I do not know, I am only sixty-five.

—Princess Metternich on when
the sex drive diminishes

My girlfriend has married an old man;
I have married younger.
Her old man is witty, sexy and strong;
Mine's the same. But mine will last longer.

—Molly Parkin

A young wife is to an old man the horse on which he rides to hell.

—Polish proverb

When I was young, I used to have success with women because I was young. Now I have successes with women because I am old. Middle age was the hardest part.

—Arthur Rubenstein

I never imagined I'd be sleeping with a sixty-year-old woman.

—Alan Simpson

I don't like aging. The only thing you get is wisdom. How many guys are sexually attracted to someone who is fifty years old?

—Grace Slick

I'm sure older guys are great lovers. But I just happen to like younger guys.

—Dottie West

The older one grows the more one likes indecency.

—Virginia Woolf

Americana

Sex gets people killed, put in jail, beaten up, bankrupted, and disgraced, to say nothing of ruined—personally, politically, and professionally. Looking for sex can lead to misfortune, and if you get lucky and find it, it can leave you maimed, infected, or dead. Other than that, it's swell; the great American pastime.

—Edna Buchanan

If he has done nothing else for American culture, he has given it two of the great lies of the twentieth century: "I buy it for the fiction" and "I buy it for the interview."

—Nora Ephron on Hugh Hefner

Women in America lead the men around by the nose, make fools of them, and the result is matriarchy. In

Europe, things are different. Men take the lead. That is as it should be.

—Sigmund Freud

Instead of fulfilling the promise of infinite orgastic bliss, sex in America of the feminine mystic is becoming a strangely joyless national compulsion, if not a contemptuous mockery.

—Betty Friedan

In the last couple of weeks I have seen the ads for the Wonder Bra. Is that really a problem in this country? Men not paying enough attention to women's breasts?

—Hugh Grant

The mammary fixation is the most infantile and most American of the sex fetishes.

—Molly Haskell

American eroticism has always been of a different provenance and complexion than the European variety, an enjoyment both furtive and bland that is closer to a blushing cartoon than a sensual celebration.

—Molly Haskell

Ninety-eight percent of American homes have TV sets . . . The people in the other two have to generate their own sex and violence.

—Franklin P. Jones

Our society treats sex as a sport, with its record breakers, its judges, its rules and its spectators.

—Susan Lydon

If American men are obsessed with money, American women are obsessed with weight. The men talk of gain, the women talk of loss, and I do not know which talk is the more boring.

—Marya Mannes

That Americans are highly sexed and that redheads are more highly sexed than others.

—W. Somerset Maugham

Europeans used to say Americans were puritanical. Then they discovered that we were not puritans. So now they say we are obsessed with sex.

—Mary McCarthy

I'm getting an abortion. I don't need one, but I feel that as an American I should exercise that right before it gets taken away.

—Betsy Salkind

I like American women. They do things sexually Russian girls would never dream of—like showering.

—Yakov Smirnoff

[Americans are] better at having a love affair that lasts ten minutes than any other people in the world.

—Stephen Spender

There's no one who's liberated to the point the American woman is and yet handles it worse. She holds her freedom like a club and beats the guy with it.

—Raquel Welch

You know how Americans are—when it comes to sex, the men can't keep from lying and the women can't keep from telling the truth.

—Robin Zander

Anatomy

I think guys like to look at tits.

—Alan Alda

She wore a short skirt and a tight sweater and her figure described a set of parabolas that could cause cardiac arrest in a yak.

—Woody Allen

There is a substantial and enlarging body of medical opinion that these deformities [small breasts] are really a disease.

—The American Society of Plastic
and Reconstructive Surgeons

No man should marry until he has studied anatomy and dissected at least one woman.

—Honoré de Balzac

Men have no idea the things women do to camouflage themselves, and once they get to [having sex], they don't care . . . They are not going to say, "Hey! Your nipples were really big in the bar!"

—Lori Barghini, inventor of the
"Silicon nipple"

Woman has ovaries, a uterus . . . It is often said that she thinks with her glands. Man superbly ignores the fact that his anatomy also includes glands, such as the testicles, and that they secrete hormones.

—Simone de Beauvoir

I'm crowding six-one. Got a mass of blond hair, sensational eyes, bluer than Newman's. Muscular but whippy, like Redford. Only trouble is I have no ass. It fell off!

—Mel Brooks

A lot of bad novels in which the clitoris is described as the red pearl and the penis is always described as engorged and throbbing.

—Rita Mae Brown on the affects of the sexual revolution

The ass is the face of the soul of sex.

—Charles Bukowski

The first time someone said, "What are your measurements?" I answered, "Thirty-seven, twenty-four, thirty-eight—but not necessarily in that order."

—Carol Burnett

Anyone who thinks that the way to a man's heart is through his stomach flunked geography.

—Robert Byrne

What's the definition of a vagina? The box a penis comes in.

—Andrew Dice Clay

You start out happy that you have no hips or boobs. All of a sudden you get them and it feels sloppy. Then just when you start liking them, they start drooping.

—Cindy Crawford

The vagina—a completely passive, receptive organ—awaits an active agent to become a functioning, excitable organ.

—Helene Deutsch

I have become the go-to guy on genitalia.

—Barney Frank on various
Washington sex scandals

Why is it that most things in the world are shaped like a man's penis?

—Whoopi Goldberg

Much like the stump-end of a whist-card pencil.

—Dr. Marian Greaves describing
the clitoris

The degree of attention which breasts receive, combined with the confusion about what the breast fetishist actually wants, makes a woman unduly anxious about them. They can never be just right; they must always be too small, too big, the wrong shape, too flabby.

—Germaine Greer

When the life of the party wants to express the idea of a pretty woman in mime, he undulates his two hands in the air and leers expressively. The notion of a curve is so closely connected to sexual semantics that some people cannot resist sniggering at road signs. The most popular image of the female . . . is all boobs and buttocks, a hallucinating sequence of parabolas and bulges.

—Germaine Greer

Biology is destiny only for girls.

—Elizabeth Hardwick

Anatomy

If I'd had breasts, I'd have ruled the world.
—Julie Harris

If anything happens to me, please arrange for me to be buried topless.
—Beatle George Harrison's mother on having breast implants at the age of seventy-three

When I was eleven, I thought that women were solid from the neck down.
—C. E. M. Joad

The penis is obviously going the way of the veriform appendix.
—Jill Johnston

Is it true what all the girls say—that you're hung like a horse?
—Peggy Hopkins Joyce, member of Ziegfeld Follies, to Charlie Chaplin

The brain is viewed as an appendage of the genital glands.
—Carl Jung on Freud's theories

The majority of states which have reviewed this issue agree they [laws concerning indecent exposure] include only genitalia.
—Julie Lewis on the legality of "mooning"

If God had wanted us to think with just our womb, why did He give us a brain?
—Clare Boothe Luce

15

In my next life, I'd like to come back five foot, two inches, with the best ass and tits you've ever seen.

—Andie MacDowell

There's an extraordinary difference between a beautiful nipple and a dull one.

—Norman Mailer

Everywhere I went, my cleavage followed. But I learned I'm not my cleavage.

—Carole Mallory

What is my favorite romantic spot? You mean in the whole world or on somebody's body?

—Jackie Mason

Our bodies are shaped to bear children and our lives are a worship of the processes of creation. All ambition and intelligence are beside that great elemental point.

—Phyllis McGinley

Imagine hanging the stones of man outside, where they are forever getting themselves knocked, pinched, and bruised. Any decent mechanic would have put them in the exact center of the body, protected by an envelop twice as thick as even a Presbyterian's skull. The elemental notion of standardization seems to have never presented itself to the celestial Edison.

—H. L. Mencken

A pair of women's breasts has more pulling power than a pair of oxen.

—Mexican proverb

Anatomy

The only place a man must come out of before he can go into.

—Frederic Mullally on the vagina

Wondrous hole! Magical hole! Dazzlingly influential hole! Noble and effulgent hole! From this hole everything follows logically: first the baby, then the placenta, then, for years and years and years until death, a way of life. It is all logic, and she who lives by the hole will also live by its logic. It is, appropriately, logic with a hole in it.

—Cynthia Ozick

Every girl should use what Mother Nature gave her before Father Time takes it away.

—Laurence J. Peter

Giving a name to the genitals may simply be an attempt to personify them but can also impute to them a life of their own, especially if their owner wishes to avoid responsibility for their actions.

—Alan Richter

Is it possible to insure my dick?

—David Lee Roth

Anyone who gives a surgeon six thousand dollars for "breast augmentation" should give some thought to investing a little more on brain augmentation.

—Mike Royko

I have a brain and a uterus, and I use them both.

—Patricia Schroeder

You know what my advice is to women about the implant situation? . . . I always feel so bad for women that couldn't afford to go the extra mile—or inch.

—Charlie Sheen

I finally found my wife's G-spot. A neighbor lady had it.

—Jim Sherbert

It was like two cement blocks hit me.

—Paul Shimkonis on his suit
against a topless bar over an
encounter with a well-built
stripper

A friend of mine got her clitoral hood pierced. I think that's disgusting. I would never do that. I'd get a clip-on.

—Sarah Silverman

If men had more up top, we'd need less up front.

—Jaci Stephen

A guy's penis is his whole life.

—Howard Stern on John Wayne
Bobbitt, whose penis was cut
off by his wife

My bust was visible under the negligée in one scene. Suddenly, there were Barbra Streisand's breasts and I was worried that people might concentrate on my body instead of my acting.

—Barbra Streisand

I've got an idea. Let's fill the whole screen with tits.

—Hunt Stromberg on a
documentary on the South
Seas

I picked my dream butt.

—Jeanne Tripplehorn on choosing
a body double for a nude
movie scene

I think, if my butt's not too big for them to be photographing it, then it shouldn't be too big for me.

—Christy Turlington

The penis is mightier than the sword.

—Mark Twain

I've met so many girls—"Here, feel these, they're brand new." You grab them and they're like bolt-ons—really hard. It's like anything—it's got to be done just right.

—Steven Tyler on breast implants

The buttocks are the most aesthetically pleasing part of the body because they are non-functional. Although they conceal an essential orifice, these pointless globes are as near the human form can ever come to abstract art.

—Kenneth Tynan

I let down my silken hair
Over my shoulders
And open my thighs
Over my lover
"Tell me, is there any part of me
that is not lovable?"

—Tzu Yeh

I'm glad I'm not a woman for a lot of reasons. Guys have a better deal . . . Getting a hard-on, that's something a woman will never understand.

—Christopher Walken

A hard man is good to find.

—Mae West

One figure can add up to a lot.

—Mae West

A curved line is the loveliest distance between two points.

—Mae West

Battle of the Sexes

Girls are so queer you never know what they mean. They say no when they mean yes, and drive a man out of his wits for the fun of it.

—Louisa May Alcott

It was an old quandary for them. He needed sex in order to feel connected to her, and she needed to feel connected to him in order to enjoy sex.

—Lisa Alther

It is not the inferiority of women that has caused their historical insignificance; it is rather their historical insignificance that has doomed them to inferiority.

—Simone de Beauvoir

If a woman gets nervous, she'll eat or go shopping. A man will attack a country—it's a whole other way of thinking.

—Elayne Boosler

There are two races of people—men and women—no matter what women's libbers would have you pretend.

Men are born with no purpose in the universe except to procreate. There's a lot of time to kill beyond that.

—Ray Bradbury

People always assume that bachelors are single by choice and spinsters because nobody asked them. It never enters their heads that poor bachelors might have worn the knees of their trousers out proposing to girls that reject them or that a girl might deliberately stay unmarried because she didn't want to spend the rest of her life filling a man's stomach with food and washing his dirty shirts.

—Jilly Cooper

Men get laid, but women get screwed.

—Quentin Crisp

Women need a reason to have sex, men just need a place.

—Billy Crystal

A hoarder of sexual grievances, a wife.

—Joan Didion

The reason husbands and wives do not understand each other is because they belong to different sexes.

—Dorothy Dix

Men are superior to women. For one thing, they can urinate from a speeding car.

—Will Durst

In general, I think it's true that women fuck to love and men love to fuck.

—Carrie Fisher

The thing women must do to rise to power is redefine their femininity. Once power was considered a masculine attribute. In fact, power has no sex.

—Katherine Graham

The real theater of the sex war is the domestic hearth.

—Germaine Greer

I'm very much in love with a woman, but I don't want her to know. If she knows I'm in love with her, she'll start treating me like shit. That's how women are.

—Arsenio Hall

In a world not made for women, criticism and ridicule follow us all the days of our lives. Usually they are indications that we are doing something right.

—Erica Jong

Throughout all of history, books were written with sperm, not menstrual blood.

—Erica Jong

Feminine passion is to masculine as an epic is to an epigram.

—Karl Kraus

Men need sexual fulfillment in order to respond to a woman emotionally; women need emotional fulfillment to respond to a man sexually.

—Ellen Krieg

No matter how much cats fight, there always seems to be plenty of kittens.

—Abraham Lincoln

I truly believe that when men are looking at women they can't see past their hooters. You could get the stupidest woman imaginable, but if she's got a beautiful pair of hooters, a man is going to want to fuck her. Whereas if I have a stupid man in front of me, I don't give a fuck how big his dick is, I want him out of my life.

—Shirley Manson

Whether women are better than men I cannot say, but I can say they are certainly no worse.

—Golda Meir

More and more it appears that, biologically, men are designed for short, brutal lives and women for long, miserable ones.

—Estelle Ramey

A man should be the head of the household. And if a woman has any brains, she can usually lead him around by the nose.

—Jane Russell

The basic conflict between men and women sexually is that men are like firemen. To us, sex is an emergency, and no matter what we're doing we can be ready in two minutes. Women are like fire. They're very exciting, but the conditions have to be exactly right for it to occur.

—Jerry Seinfeld

In real life, women are always trying to mix something up with sex—religion, or babies, or hard cash; it is only men who long for sex separated out, without rings or strings.

—Katherine Whitehorn

Remember, Ginger Rogers did everything Fred Astaire did, but she did it backwards and in high heels.

—Faith Whittlesey

On the one hand, we'll never experience childbirth. On the other hand, we can open all our own jars.

—Bruce Willis

Beauty

Life belongs to the pretty woman.

—Lady Isabel Barnett

Beauty. The power by which a woman charms a lover and terrifies a husband.

—Ambrose Bierce

Your spouse should be just attractive enough to turn you on. Anything more is trouble.

—Albert Brooks

It is better to be first with an ugly woman than the hundredth with a beauty.

—Pearl Buck

It's a good thing that beauty is only skin deep or I'd be rotten to the core.

—Phyllis Diller

A beautiful woman is paradise for the eye, the soul's hell, and purgatory for the purse.

—Estonian proverb

Beauty and folly are old companions.

—Benjamin Franklin

If Jack's in love, he's no judge of Jill's beauty.

—Benjamin Franklin

For the butterfly, mating and propagation involve the sacrifice of life; for the human being, the sacrifice of beauty.

—Johann Wolfgang von Goethe

Plain women know more about men than beautiful ones do.

—Katharine Hepburn

I've seen a lot of ugly guys in the league [National Basketball Association] with beautiful women.

—Grant Hill

Beauty without chastity, a flower without fragrance.

—Indian proverb

It's commonly known beautiful women work only on the basis of looks and not on gray matter.

—Tawny Kitaen

A woman who cannot be ugly is not beautiful.

—Karl Kraus

Pageants should be understood within the context of celebrations, as cultural harvests. We're saying, "This is the best of the young womanhood . . . the best of this year's harvest."

—Michael Marsden on beauty
pageants

25

Judgement of beauty can err, what with the wine and the dark.

—Ovid

Menstruation and childbirth are an affront to beauty and form.

—Camille Paglia

I patterned my look after Cinderella, Mother Goose and the local hooker.

—Dolly Parton

Just standing around looking beautiful is so boring, really boring.

—Michelle Pfeiffer

Let us leave the beautiful women to men with no imagination.

—Marcel Proust

In the factory we make cosmetics. In the store we sell hope.

—Charles Revson

It's not that I don't want to be a beauty, that I don't yearn to be dripping with glamour. It's just that I can't see how any woman can find time to do to herself all the things that must apparently be done to make herself beautiful.

—Cornelia Otis Skinner

Life wouldn't be worth living if we didn't have pretty women. That's natural. Any normal man likes to be around pretty women.

—Strom Thurman, on his ninety-eighth birthday

It is better to be beautiful than to be good. But it is better to be good than to be ugly.

—Oscar Wilde

A homely girl hates the mirror.

—Yiddish proverb

Birth

Yuppies have a low birth rate because they have to go to Aspen to mate.

—Dave Barry

We tried it [sex] twice and it worked both times.

—Robert Benchley

Never lend your car to anyone to whom you have given birth.

—Erma Bombeck

If men had to have babies they would only ever have one each.

—Princess Diana

If pregnancy were a book they would cut the last two chapters.

—Nora Ephron

Making love in the morning got me through morning sickness—I found I could be happy and throw up at the same time.

—Pamela Anderson Lee on being pregnant

The reproduction of mankind is a great marvel and mystery. Had God consulted me in the matter, I should have advised Him to continue the generation of the species by fashioning them out of clay.

—Martin Luther

I didn't know how babies were made until I was pregnant with my fourth child five years later.

—Loretta Lynn

My obstetrician was so dumb that when I gave birth he forgot to cut the cord. For a year that kid followed me everywhere. It was like having a dog on a leash.

—Joan Rivers

Any woman who has a child who doesn't yell is a fool. When I was having my kid it was ARRRRGH. And that was just during conception.

—Joan Rivers

I had a Jewish delivery. They knock you out at the first pain and wake you when the hairdresser shows.

—Joan Rivers

Another thing that seems quite helpful to the creative process is having babies. It does not detract at all from one's creativity. It reminds one that there is always more where that came from and there is never any shortage of ideas or of the ability to create.

—Fay Weldon

You have this myth you're sharing the birth experience. Unless you're circumcising yourself with a chain saw, I don't think so. Unless you're opening an umbrella up your ass, I don't think so.

—Robin Williams

Birth Control

... if the parts be smooth, conception is prevented. Some anoint that part of the womb on which the seed falls with oil of cedar, or with ointment of lead or with frankincense, commingled with olive oil.

—Aristotle

If instead of birth control everyone would preach drink control, you would have little poverty, less crime and fewer illegitimate children.

—Margot Asquith

He no play-a da game, he no make-a da rules.

—Earl Butz on the Pope's
position on birth control

The greatest of all contraceptives is affluence.

—Indira Gandhi

The emphasis must be not on the right to abortion but on the right to privacy and reproductive control.

—Ruth Bader Ginsburg

The pill came to market and changed the sexual and real estate habits of millions: motel chains were created to serve them.

—Herbert Gold

No glove, no love.

—Graffito

I bought a condom and put it in my wallet when I was fourteen. By the time I pulled it out to use, it was older than the girl I was with.

—Lewis Grizzard

29

There's a new medical crisis. Doctors are reporting that many men are having allergic reactions to latex condoms. They say they cause severe swelling. So what's the problem?

—Dustin Hoffman

National Condom Week is coming soon. Hey, there's a parade you don't want to miss.

—Jay Leno

In a test program, forty drugstores in Washington state will be dispensing morning-after birth control pills without prescription. In fact, men can buy them in special gift packs with cards that say, "Thanks. Maybe I'll call you sometime."

—Jay Leno

You never really know a guy until you ask him to wear a rubber.

—Madonna

I was insecure about sex. I've grown more secure. I used to use the amateur phylactics, and I only use the prophylactics now.

—Steve Martin

Contraceptives should be used on every conceivable occasion.

—Spike Milligan

Condoms aren't completely safe. A friend of mine was wearing one and got hit by a bus.

—Bob Rubin

Mrs. Sanger said the best birth control is to make your husband sleep on the roof.

—Adela Rogers St. John on feminist pioneer Margaret Sanger

Impotence and sodomy are socially okay, but birth control is flagrantly middle-class.

—Evelyn Waugh

I'm Catholic. My mother and I were unpacking and she found my diaphragm. I had to tell her it was a bathing cap for my cat.

—Lizz Winstead

I rely on my personality for birth control.

—Lizz Winstead

Condoms allow me to sleep with as many women as possible and not feel bad about it.

—Matt Zone

Bisexuality

You can't have your cake and eat it too. You can't be tied to male privilege with the right hand while clutching to your sister with the left.

—Rita Mae Brown

Well, I'm not going through life with one hand tied behind my back.

—James Dean, when asked if he was gay

31

In Europe it doesn't matter if you're a man or a woman, we make love to anyone we find attractive.

—Marlene Dietrich

I think everybody is bisexual.

—Robert Downey Jr.

I date men and I date women. What Woody Allen said was true. Say what you will about bisexuality, you have a fifty percent better chance of finding a date on Saturday night.

—David Geffen

I sleep with men and with women. I am neither queer nor not queer, nor am I bisexual.

—Allen Ginsberg

Afterwards, you know, afterwards, I often feel like being fucked by a man too.

—Joan Haggerty

Because our society is so polarized between homosexuals and heterosexuals, the bisexual closet has two doors.

—Loraine Hutchins and Lani Kaahumanu

Bisexuality is not so much a cop-out as a fearful compromise.

—Jill Johnston

Bisexuals . . . are incredibly greedy motherfuckers . . . Get off the fence and pick a hole.

—Dennis Miller

Homosexuality was invented by a straight world dealing with its own bisexuality.

—Kate Millett

When a woman comes, there's something, a sexual experience, that you cannot have when fucking a man. In the case of this girl who I was screwing—when she came there was a flooding of her uterine passage, this hot fluid, and it felt wonderful.

—Tennessee Williams

It is fatal to be a man or a woman pure and simple; one must be woman-manly or man-womanly.

—Virginia Woolf

Censorship

Won't the new "Suggested for mature audiences" protect our youngsters from such films? I don't believe so. I know many forty-five-year-old men with the mentalities of six-year-olds, and my feeling is that they should not see such pictures either.

—Shirley Temple Black

Take away the word "fuck" and you take away the right to say "fuck the government."

—Lenny Bruce

Censorship feeds the dirty mind more than the four-letter word itself.

—Dick Cavett

What progress we are making. In the Middle Ages they would have burned me. Now they are content with burning my books.

—Sigmund Freud

It is appalling that naked women cannot be kept out of the nation's living room.

—Billy Graham

Is this a book that you would ever wish your wife or servants to read?

—Mervyn Griffith-Jones, British
prosecuting attorney at
obscenity trial of D. H.
Lawrence's novel *Lady
Chatterley's Lover*

Books won't stay banned. They won't burn. Ideas don't go to jail. In the long run of history, the censor and the inquisitor have always lost. The only weapon against bad ideas is better ideas.

—Alfred Whitney Griswold

I hate to think of this sort of book getting into the wrong hands. As soon as I've finished this, I shall recommend they ban it.

—Tony Hancock

A censor is a man who knows more that he thinks you ought to.

—Granville Hicks

Censorship is the strongest drive in human nature—sex is only a weak second.

—Phil Kerby

Censorship, like charity, should begin at home; but unlike charity it should end there.

—Clare Boothe Luce

The censors say they're protecting the family unit in America when, in fact, the reality of the censorship is if you suck a tit, you're an X, but if you cut off a tit with a sword, you're GP.

—Jack Nicholson

The censors wouldn't even let me sit on a guy's lap, and I've been on more laps than a table-napkin.

—Mae West

The dirtiest book of all is the expurgated book.

—Walt Whitman

Chastity/Virginity

Made of iron, and consisting of a belt and a piece which came up under and was locked in position, so neatly made that once a woman was bridled it was out of the question for her to indulge in the gentle pleasure, as there were only a few little holes for her to piss through.

—Pierre de Bourdeille

What most men desire is a virgin who is a whore.

—Edward Dahlberg

The advantages are manifold. Not only will the purity of the virgin be maintained but the fidelity of the wife exacted. The husband will leave the wife without fear that his honor will be outraged and his affections estranged.

—French advertisement for a
chastity belt, 1880

35

Help stamp out hymens.

—Graffito

There are no chaste minds. Minds copulate wherever they meet.

—Eric Hoffer

When I was growing up, I never heard about abstinence.

—Dave Johnson

In the old days poverty kept Latin women chaste: hard work, too little sleep, these were the things that saved their humble homes from corruption.

—Juvenal

Only one woman in thousands has been endowed with the God-given aptitude to live in chastity and virginity . . . God fashioned her body so that she could be with a man, to have and rear children. No woman should be ashamed of that which God made and intended her.

—Martin Luther

Celibacy was invented by the devil.

—Martin Luther

An unattempted woman cannot boast of her chastity.

—Michel de Montaigne

She is chaste who nobody asked.

—Ovid

Virginity is a state of mind, when all's said and done.

—Mary Roberts Rinehart

Loss of virginity is rational increase; and there was never virgin got till virginity was first lost.

—William Shakespeare

The crusaders, we are told, put their wives into chastity belts before they sailed off for the Holy Land. They did not, for certain, put their own equipment out of action for the duration.

—Mary Stott

Celibacy is not hereditary.

—Oscar Wilde

In those days, young stars, male and female, were all virgins until married, and if divorced, they returned magically to that condition.

—Shelley Winters on early
Hollywood

Clothes

On edible underwear: I don't know what the big deal is about these. You wear them for a couple of days, they taste just like the other ones.

—Tom Arnold

Female clothing has been disappearing literally and philosophically.

—Marilyn Bender

You must understand that this is not a woman's dress I'm wearing. It's a man's dress.

—David Bowie on wearing a
dress while performing

Can't stand panty hose. I'm into that old, wonderful French look. Black stockings with garters.

—Mel Brooks

Briefs!

—Bill Clinton on what type of
underwear he wears

She kept the dress as a souvenir. How sick is that?

—Lucianne Goldberg on Monica
Lewinski's blue dress stained
with Bill Clinton's semen

I never wear designer things, but I'm a great supporter of women's fashion. I like to actually wear women's fashion.

—Hugh Grant

A woman takes off her claim to respect along with her garments.

—Herodotus

I don't know why I perform better as a woman; maybe the boots I wear as Norman are too heavy.

—Norman Horton who line-danced
as a man on Tuesdays and as a
woman, "Norma," on Wednesdays

I do like making boys wear my high heels and earrings. But not my panties, because that's not going to look very pretty.

—Elizabeth Hurley

When I see you wearing this tie I'll know that I am close to your heart.

—Monica Lewinsky on a gift to
Bill Clinton that he allegedly
wore before the grand jury

I would get into bed and my girlfriend would mentally
dress me.
—Richard Lewis

I hate to see an inch of flesh showing on anyone over
thirty.
—Bob Mackie

Getting paid to take my clothes off was the easiest thing
in the world.
—Marilyn Monroe

I don't know who invented the high heel, but all women
owe him a lot.
—Marilyn Monroe

As I say about girls wearing Madonna's harlot outfits, if
you advertise, you'd better be ready to sell.
—Camille Paglia

Seldom do men and women equally embrace a fashion
trend, and when they do the mutual enthusiasm lasts
only briefly. The opposite sexes like being opposites in
as many ways as possible. When French and Italian
men began to be turned on to the female leg in decora-
tive high heels, they did not like to see the same erotic
footwear on the feet of men. All but a few men stopped
wearing high heels, which went from being a man's
standard footwear to one of his favorite sexual fetishes.
—Charles Panati

The bra, or something like it, has been in use for over
6,000 years but really didn't come into its own until the
turn of the century. The first formal application for a
patent on the garment was filed on February 12, 1914

by Mary Phelps Jacob, also known as Caresse Crosby, who fashioned a prototype using some ribbons, thread, and two handkerchiefs. After World War I, the donning of the bra became synonymous with the chucking of the corset, long considered the restrainer of the female and the mainstay of her oppression. The bra allowed women to both liberate their bodies and assume a host of activities, both work and play, previously open only to men.

—Lawrence Paros

I got some new underwear the other day. Well, new to me.

—Emo Phillips

I love being a woman. You can cry. You can wear pants now. If you're on a boat and it's going to sink, you can get to go on the rescue boat first. You can wear cute clothes.

—Gilda Radner

My biggest fear is that my underwear will have a stain on it if I'm ever with a woman that I've never slept with before.

—Keanu Reeves

I don't know my Social Security number. I don't even know my bra size.

—Sharon Stone

If I don't feel like wearing a bra I don't wear one. I'd never let my nipples show at a state function—I'd be frightened the old men would have heart attacks.

—Margaret Trudeau

A dress is nothing. Fabric has no sex. Sexiness comes from the attitude applied.

—Gianni Versace

Charles Revson said women all hope to get laid, and I agree. They're sensuous. They're different from men. They dress to please men. You're not selling utility. That's why uptight women stockbrokers will put on a G-string when they get home.

—Leslie Wexner

I enjoy getting dressed as a Barbie doll.

—Vanna White

There is nothing more sensual than angora.

—Ed Wood

Hockey is a sport for white men. Basketball is a sport for black men. Golf is a sport for white men dressed like black pimps.

—Tiger Woods

Confessions

My toughest fight was with my first wife.

—Muhammad Ali

The last time I was inside a woman was when I was inside the Statue of Liberty.

—Woody Allen

Actors are all having sex with each other all the time.

—Alec Baldwin

The less I behave like Whistler's mother the night before, the more I look like her the morning after.

—Tallulah Bankhead

I was very hungry in my younger days. Starving. Out of my mind . . . I'd just think, "What a waste of time, not being a slut!"

—Kim Basinger

I'm just a person trapped inside a woman's body.

—Elayne Boosler

I wish my butt did not go sideways, but I guess I have to face that.

—Christie Brinkley

I'm fourteen years old sexually—and it's terrific.

—Mel Brooks

My kid had sex with your honor student.

—Bumper sticker

I'm not a great lover, but at least I'm fast.

—Drew Carey

I always wanted to be an animated character. And basically that's what I do now. I'm kind of an X-rated Cinderella.

—Cher

In my younger days, I used to pick up sluts, and I don't mean that nastily.

—Kevin Costner

I need sex for a clear complexion, but I'd rather do it for love.

—Joan Crawford

I've never even spent a whole night in bed with a woman. Never. When it was time to sleep, either they'd go home or I'd fall asleep on the couch or the floor.

—Sammy Davis Jr.

I'm so ugly I can't even get raped.

—Phyllis Diller

One of my cousins sucked my dick when I was nine. It was for about four seconds, and I said I would do it back to him, but I reneged.

—Robert Downey Jr.

I'm wild, I don't care—I love sex.

—Amy Fisher

I do not want to be the world's greatest lover.

—Clark Gable

If I'm not dropping air biscuits, something's wrong . . . Love me, love my farts.

—Whoopi Goldberg

When I have sex it takes four minutes. And that includes dinner and a show.

—Gilbert Gottfried

I'll fuck anything that moves.

—Dennis Hopper, as Frank Booth in *Blue Velvet*

My girlfriend always laughs during sex no matter what she's reading.

—Steve Jobs

In most artists there's a self-destructive streak. Drugs, sex, and doomed liaisons were my form of destruction.

—Elton John

I'm a bit of a prude myself.

—Gypsy Rose Lee

All I can say is if they show my butt in a movie, it better be a wide shot.

—Jennifer Lopez

All I have to do is lick my finger, stick it up in the air, and shit sticks to it.

—Courtney Love

I donated my tits to Cher. And she was so glad to get them I can't even tell you.

—Bette Midler

They weren't shooting all those sexy movies just to sell peanut butter. They wanted to sample the merchandise.

—Marilyn Monroe on sex with
movie studio executives

My image has been the wholesome girl-next-door, apple-cheek thing . . . Behind this facade, this body is a mass of hickeys.

—Ann Murray

I don't like to admit it, but if a girl baited her trap with sex, she'd catch me every time—and it's unlikely this will ever cease to work.

—Willie Nelson

I don't go through an hour a day when I don't get turned on.

—Jack Nicholson

I still like to pee off the porch every now and then. There's nothing like peeing on those snobs in Beverly Hills.

—Dolly Parton

I like fucking . . . I separate love from sex.

—Roman Polanski

Basically, I'm like a whore. I'll give people whatever they want so they like me.

—Christina Ricci

I only put clothes on so that I'm not naked when I go out shopping.

—Julia Roberts

Many times while I was getting laid, in my head I was doing a business deal.

—Arnold Schwarzenegger

I had sex with a woman I shouldn't have, OK? And she was a prostitute.

—Jerry Springer

I fucking love women. I definitely got out of control in that arena, and I still have out-of-control binges in Vegas and shit.

—Matt Stone

I do, and I also wash and iron them.

—Dennis Thatcher, husband of
British Prime Minister when
asked who wears the pants in
his family

We had more fun fighting than most couples do making love.

—Michael Todd on his
relationship with his wife,
Elizabeth Taylor

I am a source of satisfaction to him, a nurse, a piece of furniture, a woman—nothing more.

—Sophie Tolstoy

If it's on the dress, he must confess.

—James A. Traficon Jr. on Monica
Lewinsky's blue dress stained
with Bill Clinton's semen

I write to be sexually desirable.

—Kenneth Tynan

I didn't like fucking then and I still don't—it's dull.

—Sid Vicious

I know the difference between a good man and a bad one, but I haven't decided which I like better.

—Mae West

My boobs are too saggy, and the kids call me "Weenie Butt."

—Tammy Wynette

Dating

Sometimes it's Britney Spears and sometimes it's Carrie Fisher. I can't tell if I've got a Lolita complex or an Oedipus complex.

—Ben Affleck on his love life

Plenty of guys are good in bed, but conversation, now there's an art.

—Linda Barnes

Will had to reluctantly admit that was true, which certainly helped him with dates since then.

—Roy Black, friend of William
Kennedy Smith, on Smith's
having sex twice in thirty
minutes with Patricia Bowman,
who claimed she was raped

It's terrific if you're a computer.

—Rita Mae Brown on what she
thought of computer dating

One woman I was dating said, "Come on over, there's nobody home." I went over—nobody was home.

—Rodney Dangerfield

It's too much trouble to get laid. Because you have to go out with a guy, and go to dinner with him, and listen to him talk about his opinions. And I don't have that kind of time.

—Kathy Griffin

Girls usually fall over themselves to go out with me.
—George Harrison

I've never seen black men with fine white women. They be ugly, mugly dogs.
—Spike Lee

I once dated a guy who drank coffee and alcohol at the same time. What a prince. Bad breath, limp dick, and wouldn't go to sleep.
—Kris McGaha

Men generally pay for all expenses on a date . . . Either sex, however, may bring a little gift, its value to be determined by the bizarreness of the sexual request to be made later that evening.
—P. J. O'Rourke

Is it bad when you refer to all porno magazines as "dates?"
—Patton Oswalt

Going to a stranger's apartment on the first date . . . should correctly be interpreted as consent to sex.
—Camille Paglia

A man on a date wonders if he'll get lucky. The woman already knows.
—Monica Piper

The 3-F's of dating: One: Film. Two: Food. Three: Fuck.
—Kevin Pollak on the bachelor's credo

It wasn't that no one asked me to the prom, it was that no one would tell me where it was.

—Rita Rudner

A date is a job interview that lasts all night. The only difference between a date and a job interview is that there are not many job interviews where there's a chance you'll end up naked at the end of it.

—Jerry Seinfeld

I broke up with my girlfriend. She moved in with another guy, and I draw the line at that.

—Garry Shandling

On a date . . . I wonder if there is going to be any sex— and if I'm going to be involved.

—Garry Shandling

Dr. Ruth says we women should tell our lovers how to make love to us. My boyfriend goes nuts if I tell him how to drive.

—Pam Stone

I went out with this one guy; I was very excited about it. He took me out to dinner, he made me laugh—he made me pay. He's like, "Oh, I'm sorry. I forgot my wallet." "Really? I forgot my vagina."

—Lisa Sundstedt

I will not go out with a man who wears more jewelry than me, and I'll never go to bed with a guy who calls me Babe. Other than that, however, I'm real flexible.

—Linda Sunshine

Employees make the best dates. You don't have to pick them up and they're always tax deductible.

—Andy Warhol

We have a very beautiful but strange relationship. We don't worry about who the other dates.

—Tammy Wynette on
Burt Reynolds

Death

Sex is exciting only when it is a subtle and pervasive part of the relationship between men and women, varying in its form from adolescence to old age, and it dies only with death if it is properly nourished in life.

—Pearl Buck

Sexual intercourse is kicking death in the ass while singing.

—Charles Bukowski

The rich widow cries with one eye and rejoices with the other.

—Miguel de Cervantes Saavedra

When you don't have any money, the problem is food. When you have money, it's sex. When you have both, it's health. If everything is simply jake, then you're frightened of death.

—J. P. Donleavy

Honey, sex doesn't stop until you're in the grave.

—Lena Horne

How alike are the groans of love to those of the dying.

—Malcolm Lowry

I think of sex as a very important thing, like birth or death.

—Henry Miller

When I have one foot in the grave I will tell the truth about women. I shall tell it, jump into my coffin, pull the lid over me and say, "Do what you like now."

—Leo Tolstoy

When he is late for dinner and I know he must be either having an affair or lying dead in the street, I always hope he's dead.

—Judith Viorst

Sex feels good, Jim Beam tastes good, but cocaine will kill your ass.

—Hank Williams Jr. on a star's lifestyle

Divorce

A wife lasts only for the length of the marriage, but an ex-wife is there for the rest of your life.

—Woody Allen

I'm not upset about my divorce. I'm only upset that I'm not a widow.

—Roseanne Barr

Alimony is like putting gas into another guy's car.

—Milton Berle

I've never been married, but I tell people I'm divorced so they won't think something's wrong with me.
—Elayne Boosler

Divorce is the one human tragedy that reduces everything to cash.
—Rite Mae Brown

Fission after fusion.
—Rita Mae Brown

The two most common causes of divorce? Men and women.
—Eddie Cantor

It wasn't exactly a divorce. I was traded.
—Tim Conway

So many persons think divorce a panacea for every ill, who find out when they try it, that the remedy is worse than the disease.
—Dorothy Dix

Divorce is the sacrament of adultery.
—French proverb

If divorce has increased one thousand percent, don't blame the women's movement. Blame the obsolete sex roles on which our marriages were based.
—Betty Friedan

The happiest time of anyone's life is just after the first divorce.
—John Kenneth Galbraith

In our family we don't divorce men—we bury them.
—Ruth Gordon

Divorce? No. Murder? Yes.

> —Anne Hayes on whether she
> ever considered divorce

Anonymous desertion: the poor man's method of divorce.

> —Max Kauffmann

Being divorced is like being hit by a Mack truck. If you live through it, you start looking very carefully to the right and to the left.

> —Jean Kerr

More divorces start in the bedroom than in any other room in the house.

> —Ann Landers

It's really lawyers that make divorces nasty. You know, if there was a nice ceremony like getting married for divorce, it'd be much better.

> —John Lennon

Love is generally valued at its highest during two periods in life: during the days of courting and the days in court.

> —Lee Marvin

If the income tax is the price you have to pay to keep the government on its feet, alimony is the price we have to pay for sweeping a woman off hers.

> —Groucho Marx

If you made a list of the reasons why any couple got married, and another list of the reasons for their divorce, you'd have a hell of a lot of overlapping.

> —Mignon McLaughlin

A husband may sue for a divorce on account of the wife's adultery. A wife may sue for divorce only in the case in which the husband introduces a permanent mistress into the marital household.

—Napoleon

What scares me about divorce is that my children might put me in a home for unwed mothers.

—Teressa Skelton

Instead of getting married again, I'm going to find a woman I don't like and just give her a house.

—Rod Stewart

The biggest cause of divorce is marriage.

—Travis Tritt

I'm getting a divorce and dating a much younger woman. There's no way I can keep my wife and girlfriend happy at the same time.

—Ted Turner

Henry VIII . . . didn't get divorced, he just had [his wives'] heads chopped off when he got tired of them. That's a good way to get rid of a woman—no alimony!

—Ted Turner

Both of my ex-wives closed their eyes when making love because they didn't want to see me having a good time.

—Joseph Wambaugh

Ah, yes, divorce . . . From the Latin word meaning to rip a man's genitals through his wallet.

—Robin Williams

Exercise

Good sex is absolutely wonderful for you—much better than jogging.

—Jilly Cooper

We do this because we want our guys to find us attractive.

—Jane Fonda on women working out

She didn't like to wrestle, but you should see her box.

—Graffito

Golf is the most fun you can have without taking your clothes off.

—Chi Chi Rodriguez

People who train are very sexual—you clean your body from the inside, you regenerate your cells.

—Jean-Claude Van Damme

There are basically two types of exercise in Hollywood these days: jogging and helping a recently divorced friend move.

—Robert Wagner

Fame

The easiest kind of relationship for me is with ten thousand people. The hardest is with one.

—Joan Baez

Sometimes I have this dream that I'd like to walk naked down the street and leave all my fame behind.

—Kim Basinger

I'm a rock star! I have a big cock.
—David Bowie

I signed a pussy lip once.

—Jerry Cantrell

I have found that it [fame] doesn't get you laid, and you don't get as much free stuff as you'd think.
—Anthony Edwards

If that man becomes president, I'll never have to work again.
—Gennifer Flowers on her new
celebrity resulting from her
relationship with Bill Clinton

Elton's already a queen, so isn't this a bit of a comedown?
—Boy George on Elton John
being knighted

Fame is a powerful aphrodisiac.
—Graham Greene

It was like a case of premature ejaculation. Over in a flash and deeply unsatisfying.
—Glenn Matlock on his short
membership in the British rock
band, the Sex Pistols

Supermodels, with legs up to their shoulders . . . kept coming and praising me. I said to my wife, "If this had happened thirty years ago, I'd be dead of whisky and fornication."
—Frank McCourt on winning a
Pulitzer Prize

The show is my escape valve. When I tear off my shirt and gyrate my pelvis . . . That just shows how repressed I am—a guy who wants to push his sex at the lens but can only do it as a joke.

—Conan O'Brien

We got the rock star fever by then—limousines everywhere, groupies sucking our dicks, dealers dropping by with bags of white powder.

—Ozzy Osbourne

I get very sexually excited on stage. It's like making love to nine thousand people at once.

—Prince

Being famous is like [a girl] having big tits. People always stare at you.

—Chris Rock

You can be as ugly as I am and still get laid more than the best-looking guy. Because I'm in KISS.

—Gene Simmons

Basically, as a rock star, your nearest equivalent in history is a Roman emperor. You have enough money to fill a room with cocaine and women and drink. You can debauch yourself to death.

—Sting

Families

If God wanted sex to be fun, He wouldn't have included children as a punishment.

—Ed Bluestone

I have a lot of friends who are bringing up their children alone. Men are not a necessity. You don't need them to live. You don't have to have them to survive.

—Cher

If the vice president thinks it's disgraceful for an unmarried woman to bear a child, and if he believes that a woman cannot adequately raise a child without a father, then he'd better make sure abortion remains safe and legal.

—Diane English, creator of
television show *Murphy Brown*

The message about sex and relationships that she had gotten as a child was confused, contradictory. Sex was for men, and marriage, like lifeboats, was for women and children.

—Carrie Fisher

Incest, a game the whole family can play.

—Graffito

As long as fathers rule and do not nurture, as long as mothers nurture and do not rule, the conditions favoring the development of father-daughter incest will prevail.

—Judith Lewis Herman

Most mothers think that to keep young people away from lovemaking it is enough never to speak of it in their presence.

—Marie La Fayette

They fuck you up, your mum and dad.

—Philip Larkin

Don't bother discussing sex with small children. They rarely have anything to add.

—Fran Lebowitz

I get this for the rest of my life. Yes! Mom is a happy camper.

—Pamela Anderson Lee on
husband Tommy's penis

Come, let us make our father drink wine, and we will lie with him, that we may preserve seed of our father.

—Lot's daughter, Genesis 19:32

Kids, they're not easy, but there has to be some penalty for sex.

—Bill Maher

The fact of the matter is that the prime responsibility of a woman is to be on earth long enough to find the best mate possible for herself, and conceive children who will improve the species.

—Norman Mailer

It doesn't help matters when prime time TV has Murphy Brown—a character who supposedly epitomizes today's intelligent, highly paid, professional woman—mocking the importance of fathers by bearing a child alone and calling it just another "lifestyle choice."

—Dan Quayle

My husband and I are either going to buy a dog or have a child. We can't decide whether to ruin our carpet or ruin our lives.

—Rita Rudner

When the wife wants the husband to stay at home, she talks less and cleans more.

—Yiddish proverb

Fantasies

My wife said her wildest sexual fantasy would be if I got my own apartment.

—Rodney Dangerfield

In my sex fantasy, nobody loves me for my mind.

—Nora Ephron

What a man enjoys about a woman's clothes are his fantasies of how she would look without them.

—Brendan Francis

When two people make love, there are at least four people present—the two who are actually there and the two they are thinking about.

—Sigmund Freud

Bill Clinton's gorgeous. I'd love to sleep with him.

—Boy George

I know I have low self-esteem. When we were in bed together, I would fantasize that I was someone else.

—Richard Lewis

. . . even if it wasn't good, she could fake it the best.

—Keanu Reeves on his fantasy to
have sex with Meryl Streep

My big fantasy is to seduce a priest.

—Linda Ronstadt

I feel sexy a whole lot of the time. That's one of the reasons I'm in this job: to exercise my sexual fantasies. When I'm on stage, it's like doing it with twenty thousand of your closest friends.

—David Lee Roth

You don't always get a chance to fuck when you're horny or punch somebody in the face when you feel like it . . . When people become disenchanted with the world, they turn to fantasy—and here we [KISS] are.

—Gene Simmons

How can it be the fuck of the century when a woman has to pretend to have three orgasms in four minutes from anatomically incorrect positions? I mean, that's a total male fantasy.

—Sharon Stone on a movie scene

First Times

I was alone at the time.

—Woody Allen

I can remember the night I lost my innocence in the back seat of the family car. It would have been more memorable if I hadn't been alone.

—Red Buttons

I wasn't the least bit satisfied.

—Cher on her claim that Warren Beatty took her virginity when she was sixteen

I was seventeen and making *Shampoo* [when Warren Beatty] offered to relieve me of the huge burden of my virginity . . . I decided against it.

—Carrie Fisher

Somehow we fell into bed together, without understanding why.

—Grace Kelly on losing her virginity

A youth with his first cigar makes himself sick—a youth with his first girl makes other people sick.

—Mary Wilson Little

The idea that the first guy I ever slept with, my lover when I was fifteen, is married and has kids really breaks me up. I wonder if he still loves me. He probably does.

—Madonna

Oh, about twenty-one.

—Dennis Rodman on how old he was when he lost his virginity

Receiving this honor is without a question one of the greatest moments of my life, second only to that magical evening, backstage in Shelley Winters' dressing room, where I first became a man.

—Martin Short upon receiving an honorary doctorate degree

I found myself thinking it was a bit like my disappointment when I was confirmed. This may be blasphemous but I think not. For expecting to achieve union with God is similar to expecting to achieve it with man. Only I minded much more as regards man.

—Dodie Smith

I did it with as much excitement as I felt the first time I made love some forty-two years ago.

—Ted Turner on a business deal

Men always want to be a woman's first love, women like to be a man's last romance.

—Oscar Wilde

Food

The right diet directs sexual energy into the parts that matter.

—Barbara Cartland

As a rule, they're the most incredibly warm people. If making love to you was going to make you happy, they'd make love. If you were tired and didn't want to make it, they'd cook you a meal and make you feel at home. They really were ports of call.

—Eric Clapton on groupies

When my wife has sex with me there's always a reason. One night she used me to time an egg.

—Rodney Dangerfield

The main problem with marriage is that, for a man, sex is hunger—like eating. If a man is hungry and can't get to a fancy French restaurant, he'll go to a hot dog stand. For a woman, what's important is love and romance.

—Joan Fontaine

Whenever I want a really nice meal, I start dating again.

—Susan Healey

It's no longer sex, drugs and rock and roll. Today it's food, wine and sex—and an occasional cigar.

—Emeril Lagasse

Britain is the only country in the world where the food is more dangerous than the sex.

—Jackie Mason

Love and eggs should be fresh to be enjoyed.

—Russian proverb

The only premarital thing girls don't do these days is cooking.

—Omar Sharif

When men reach their sixties and retire, they go to pieces. Women go right on cooking.

—Gail Sheehy

My sister was with two men in one night. She could hardly walk after that. Can you imagine? Two dinners!

—Sarah Silverman

My uncle Murray said, "You're a man if you can make love as long as it takes to cook a chicken."

—David Steinberg

If a guy cooks a gal dinner, he's going to be slept with, eventually.

—Jay Thomas

You sleep with a guy once, and, before you know it, he wants to take you to dinner.

—Myers Yori

Gossip

Paula Jones did not want her children to grow up thinking their mother was a slut.

—Gil Davis, Jones's lawyer, on
why she filed a sexual
harassment lawsuit against
Bill Clinton

We women as naturally love a scandal as you men do debauchery; and we can no more keep up conversation without one, than you can live an age without t'other.

—Mary Davys

Men have always detested woman's gossip because they suspect the truth: their measurements are being taken and compared.

—Erica Jong

She bad-mouthed me when we broke up. She said I faked foreplay.

—Richard Lewis

People don't like to talk about sex, they just like to do it.

—Frank Mankiewicz on the
Clinton-Lewinsky scandal

She's afraid that if she leaves, she'll become the life of the party.

—Groucho Marx on a starlet

If all the girls attending it [the Yale prom] were laid end to end, I wouldn't be surprised.

—Dorothy Parker

As I grow older and older
And totter towards the tomb
I find that I care less and less
Who goes to bed with whom.

—Dorothy L. Sayers

She's the kind of girl who climbed the ladder of success, wrong by wrong.

—Mae West

Health

A psychiatrist asks a lot of expensive questions your wife asks for nothing.

—Joey Adams

I thought I had PMS, but my doctor said, "I've got good news and bad news. The good news is, you don't have PMS. The bad news is, you're a bitch."

—Rhonda Bates

The total deprivation of sex produces irritability.

—Dr. Elizabeth Blackwell

I told my wife that there was a chance that radiation might hurt my reproductive organs, but she said in her opinion it's a small price to pay.

—Johnny Carson

The best cure for hypochondria is to forget about your own body and get interested in someone else's.

—Ace Goodman

The first sexual stirrings of little girls, so mashed, so complex, so foolish as compared with the sex of little boys.

—Lillian Hellman

If men could get pregnant, abortion would be a sacrament.

—Florynce R. Kennedy

The women who got implants sued Dow Corning because they felt betrayed by the implant company. Betrayed? What, you mean I can't put a petroleum by-product in a baggie and insert it in my chest cavity? I am shocked! And betrayed!

—Dani Klein

They are like two balls of burning flame.

—Pamela Anderson Lee on pain
from removing breast implants

I have a tremendous fear of intimacy. I feel lucky just to get aroused, because my penis is usually in the shape of a question mark. If I'm lucky enough to get an erection, fortunately for me, my hard-on points to the nearest counseling center.

—Richard Lewis

No position is impossible when you are young and healthy.

—Joe Orton

PMS ain't nothing compared to going on a diet.

—Dolly Parton

Caucasian? It was on my army draft card. I thought it meant circumcised.

—Elvis Presley

I can't wait to get Alzheimer's—new pussy every night!

—Bobby Slayton

[If men menstruated] sanitary supplies would be federally funded and free. Of course, some men would still pay for the prestige of such commercial brands as Paul Newman Tampons, Muhammad Ali's Rope-A-Dope Pads, John Wayne Maxi Pads, and Joe Namath Jock Shields—"For those light bachelor days."

—Gloria Steinem

I have more trouble getting a prescription for Valium than I do having my uterus lowered and made into a penis.

—Lily Tomlin

He may be fat, stupid and old, but nonetheless he can condemn the woman's flabby body and menopause and encounter only sympathy if he exchanges her for a younger one.

—Liv Ullman

The mind of a post-menopausal woman is virtually uncharted territory.

—Barbara G. Walker

Homophobia

If homosexuals are a legitimate minority group, so are nail biters, dieters, fat people, short people and murderers.

—Anita Bryant

He is purple—the gay pride color; and his antenna is
shaped like a triangle—the gay pride symbol.

—Jerry Falwell warning parents
that "Teletubby" Tinky Winky
is gay

I have nothing against gays and lesbians. I have lots of
gay boys working for me.

—Zsa Zsa Gabor

It's funny how heterosexuals have lives and the rest of
us have "lifestyles."

—Sonia Johnson

The Bible contains six admonishments to homosexuals
and 362 admonishments to heterosexuals. That doesn't
mean that God doesn't love heterosexuals. It's just that
they need more supervision.

—Lynn Lavner

The radical right is so homophobic that they're blaming
global warming on the AIDS quilt.

—Dennis Miller

This sort of thing may be tolerated by the French—but
we are British, thank God.

—Viscount Montgomery on
homosexuality

I have this nightmare I go to Hollywood and find out Mr.
T is a faggot.

—Eddie Murphy

I'd rather be black than gay because when you're black
you don't have to tell your mother.

—Charles Pierce

Gay Republicans—how exactly does that work? We disapprove of our own lifestyle. We beat ourselves up in parking lots.

—Paula Poundstone

If homosexuality is a disease, let's all call in queer to work. "Hello, can't work today, still queer."

—Robin Tyler

When I was in the military they gave me a medal for killing two men and a discharge for loving one.

—On a Vietnam veteran's
tombstone

Homosexuality

Lesbianism is far more than a sexual preference: it is a political stance.

—Sidney Abbott

Feminism is a theory, lesbianism is a practice.

—Ti-Grace Atkinson

Homosexuality is God's way of insuring that the truly gifted aren't burdened with children.

—Sam Austin

The male party line concerning lesbians is that women become lesbians out of reaction to men. This is a pathetic illustration of the male ego's inflated proportions. I became a lesbian because of women, because women are beautiful, strong and compassionate.

—Rita Mae Brown

This is a celebration of individual freedom, not of homosexuality. No government has the right to tell its citizens when or whom to love. The only queer people are those who don't love anybody.

—Rita Mae Brown

I started being really proud of the fact that I was gay even though I wasn't.

—Kurt Cobain

How the fuck do I know if Joan was a dyke?

—Bette Davis on Joan Crawford

I discarded a whole book because the leading character wasn't on my wavelength. She was a lesbian with doubts about her masculinity.

—Peter De Vries

I am the love that dare not speak its name.

—Lord Alfred Douglas

Lesbianism has always seemed to me an extremely inventive response to the shortage of men but otherwise not worth the trouble.

—Nora Ephron

Homosexuality is assuredly no advantage, but it is nothing to be ashamed of, no vice, no degradation; it cannot be classified as an illness.

—Sigmund Freud

Old fairies never die, they merely blow away.

—Graffito

I am absolutely convinced that if everyone would come out at once and stay out we could put an end to most of our problems.

—Barbara Grier

Want to know why girls turn from straight to gay? Because the sex is great.

—Anne Heche

Up until that point, that was the best sex I'd ever had.

—Anne Heche on sex with
Ellen DeGeneres

If I was gay, I swear I would say it, but I ain't never liked a woman in my bed, I swear to God.

—Whitney Houston

Love between women is seen as a paradigm of love between equals, and that is perhaps its greatest attraction.

—Elizabeth Janeway

Give me a couple of drinks and I'll be the bitch.

—Elton John

I never said I was a dyke even to a dyke because there wasn't a dyke in the land who thought she should be a dyke or even thought she was a dyke so how could we talk about it?

—Jill Johnston

My cousin is an agoraphobic homosexual, which makes it kind of hard for him to come out of the closet.

—Bill Kelly

If you removed all the homosexuals and homosexual influence from what is generally regarded as American culture, you would be pretty much left with *Let's Make a Deal.*

—Fran Lebowitz

Men are weak and constantly need reassurance, so now that they fail to find adulation in the opposite sex, they're turning to each other. Less and less do men need women. More and more do gentlemen prefer gentlemen.

—Anita Loos, author of
Gentlemen Prefer Blondes

I'm not a lesbian, but I thought it was undignified to say so. I'm not going to say that I've never slept with a woman, but I love men.

—Madonna

There is nothing mysterious or magic about lesbian lovemaking . . . The mystery and the magic come from the person with whom you are making love.

—Del Martin and Phyllis Lyon

If boys are better, why should a male choose to love an inferior female? If a penis is so great, two penises should be even greater. In large and small ways, boys are actually conditioned against heterosexuality because society is so relentlessly for masculinity.

—Letty Cottin Pogrebin

People think you're a lesbian because you can't get a man. Then explain to me why the only times in my life I've slept with men was when I couldn't get a woman.

—Georgia Ragsdale

I resent like hell that I was maybe eighteen before I ever heard the "L" word. It would have made all the difference for me had I grown up knowing that the reason I didn't fit in was because they hadn't told me there were more categories to fit into.

—Michelle Shocked

With overpopulation an imminent threat to civilized life, the only valid reason for disapproving of queers has vanished. We ought to encourage them.

—Kenneth Tynan

I have no doubt that lesbianism makes a woman virile and open to any sexual stimulation, and that she is more often than not a more adequate and lively partner in bed than a "normal woman."

—Charlotte Wolff

Horniness

Females are naturally libidinous, incite the males to copulation, and cry out during the act of coition.

—Aristotle

My inspiration is right below my waist and in between my legs.

—Jon Bon Jovi

You cannot fight lust if you do not flee from the presence of men.

—Caesaria

You know that look women get when they want sex? Me neither.

—Drew Carey

That's all I can remember—thinking about getting laid, getting blown . . . I was twenty-one years old, my dick was always hard, and they were so willing.

—David Cassidy

The man's desire is for the woman; the woman's desire is for the desire of the man.

—Samuel Taylor Coleridge

From the moment I was six, I felt sexy. And let me tell you it was hell, sheer hell, waiting to do something about it.

—Bette Davis

I'm obsessed with girls. When you're my age your hormones are just kicking in and there's not much besides sex on your mind.

—Leonardo DiCaprio

The desire engendered in the male gland is a hundred times more difficult to control than the desire bred in the female glands. All girls agreeing to a lovers' tête-à-tête in a car, knowing that they will limit their actions to arousing desires and then defend their "virtue," should be horsewhipped.

—Marlene Dietrich

I could not get over her butt, so I married her.

—Robert Downey Jr. on
Deborah Falconer

Anyone can be passionate, but it takes real lovers to be silly.

—Rose Franklin

The average male thinks about sex every eleven minutes while he's awake.

—Dr. Patrick Greene

It's ill-becoming for an old broad to sing about how bad she wants it. But occasionally we do.

—Lena Horne

Whatsamatter honey? You sit in a puddle, or you just glad to see me?

—Holly Hughes

A bit of lusting after someone does wonders for you and is good for your skin.

—Elizabeth Hurley about her favorite deadly sin

You say, "Good morning," and she wants to make love. You say, "Good afternoon," and she wants to make love. You say, "Good night," and she wants to make love.

—Don Johnson on wife Melanie Griffith

I'm looking for a woman with an intense sexual appetite, because I don't ever want to have to cheat.

—David Keith

The sacrilegious truth is, my sex drive diminished sharply when I started skipping periods, and vanished entirely as soon as they stopped for good. Now the only thing I miss about sex is the cigarette afterward.

—Florence King

Everything which inflames one's appetite is likely to arouse the other also. Pepper, mustard, ketchup and

Worcestershire sauce—shun them all. And even salt, in any but the smallest quantity, is objectionable; it is such a goad toward carnalism that the ancient fable depicted Venus as born of the salt of sea-wave.

—Dr. Dio Lewis on women
in 1874

Everyone probably thinks I'm a raving nymphomaniac, that I have an insatiable sexual appetite, when the truth is I'd rather read a book.

—Madonna

The ability to enjoy your sex life is central. I don't give a shit about anything else. My obsession is total. What else is there to live for?

—Dudley Moore

It's a mess ain't it? He's a horny little toad.

—Dolly Parton on Bill Clinton

Men wake up aroused in the morning. We can't help it. We just wake up and we want you. And the women are thinking, "How can you want me the way I look in the morning?" It's because we can't see you. We have no blood anywhere near our optic nerve.

—Andy Rooney

Men only have two feelings—we're either hungry or horny. I tell my wife, if I don't have an erection, make me a sandwich.

—Bobby Slayton

Sometimes I look at a cute guy and get a uterus twinge.

—Carrie Snow

Of the delights of this world man cares most for sexual intercourse. He will go to any length for it—risk fortune, character, reputation, life itself.

—Mark Twain

Lust is what makes you keep wanting to do it, even when you have no desire to be with each other. Love is what makes you keep wanting to be with each other, even when you have no desire to do it.

—Judith Viorst

I think I could fall madly in bed with you.

—Jimmy Williams

Impotence/Frigidity

The female is, as it were, an impotent male, for it is through a certain incapacity that the female is female, being incapable of concocting the nutriment [menstrual fluid] into semen because of the coldness of her nature.

—Aristotle

When I look at the prism of life and I notice that the guy in the commercial is about ten years younger than I am, that is not very settling.

—Tom Brokaw on the drug Viagra

An erection is a mysterious thing. There's always that fear, each time one goes, that you won't be seeing it again.

—Kirk Douglas

To succeed with the opposite sex, tell her you're impotent. She can't wait to disprove it.

—Cary Grant

The tragedy is when you've got sex in the head instead of down where it belongs.

—D. H. Lawrence

Women think of being a man as a gift. It is a duty. Even making love can be a duty. A man has always got to get it up and love isn't always enough.

—Norman Mailer

The latest news on this new impotency drug Viagra. Some insurance companies won't pay unless men can prove that they're impotent. Which means that men are at a disadvantage if they have a really hot pharmacist.

—Conan O'Brien

I hate a women who offers herself because she ought to do so, and, cold and dry, thinks of her sewing when she's making love.

—Ovid

At my age, one becomes terrified of impotence. But I know I shall never cease to be sensual—even on my death bed. If the doctor is young and handsome, I shall draw him into my arms.

—Tennessee Williams

Infidelity/Adultery

It is as absurd to say that a man can't love one woman all the time as it is to say that a violinist needs several violins to play the same piece of music.

—Honoré de Balzac

My wife is married. I'm not.

—Charles Barkley

I'm not telling everybody, "If you're not happy, go out and screw around because your wife will become a dynamo for you," but I got to be honest with you, that's what happened to me.

—Garth Brooks

Affairs are all right. Just be insanely careful not to have your husband find out.

—Helen Gurley Brown

Never tell. Not if you love your wife . . . In fact, if your old lady walks in on you deny it. Yeah. Just flat out lie and she'll believe it: I'm telling ya. This chick came downstairs with a sign around her neck: "Lay on top of me or I'll die."

—Lenny Bruce

Baloney!

—Barbara Bush on allegations that husband George had an affair

It's very disappointing and hurtful. How come nobody ever thought I had an affair with anyone?

—Barbara Bush on Washington scandals

Do infants enjoy infancy as much as adults enjoy adultery?

—George Carlin

The woman who is adulterous in her own home must always remember one thing—put the seat down.

—William Cole

He had lied to me. The bastard was cheating on me—
with his wife!

—Joan Collins on producer
George England

I keep the Commandments, I love my neighbor as myself, and to avoid coveting my neighbor's wife, I desire
to be coveted by her: which you know is quite another
thing.

—William Congreve

An affair now and then is good for a marriage. It adds
spice, stops it from getting boring. I ought to know.

—Bette Davis

Mistresses we keep for pleasure, concubines for daily
attendance upon our persons, wives to bear us legitimate children and to be our faithful housekeepers.

—Demosthenes

I want to have a baby, and I want Peter Jennings to be
the father . . . I know he's married, but we could just
have a cheap and tawdry affair.

—Sheena Easton

A cuckold is the husband of an unfaithful wife—a far
nastier and more humiliating state, apparently, than
being the wife of a philanderer, for which in fact no
word exists.

—Anne Faust-Sterling

Thou shall not commit adultery . . . Unless in the mood.

—W. C. Fields

Where there's marriage without love, there will be love without marriage.

—Benjamin Franklin

Adultery is in your heart not only when you look with excessive sexual desire at a woman who is not your wife, but also if you look in the same manner at your wife.

—Pope John Paul II

He [Tammy Wynette's husband] sued for divorce on the most serious grounds of all—adultery. I didn't think that was fair. Tammy wasn't wearing his ring the first time she and I made love. I had taken it off her personally.

—George Jones

If I ever want to have an affair with a married man again, especially if he's the president, please shoot me.

—Monica Lewinsky

Some people claim that marriage interferes with romance. There's no doubt about it. Anytime you have a romance, your wife is bound to interfere.

—Groucho Marx

Eighty percent of married men cheat in America. The rest cheat in Europe.

—Jackie Mason

Whosoever looketh on a woman to lust after her, hath committed adultery with her already in his heart.

—Matthew 5:28

I think a man can have two, maybe three affairs while he is married. But three is the absolute maximum. After that, you are cheating.

—Yves Montand

Never be unfaithful to a lover, except with your wife.

—P. J. O'Rourke

Should a man in private be without control or guidance in his pleasures and commit some indiscretion with a prostitute or servant girl, the wife should not take it hard or be angry, reasoning that because of his respect for her, he does not include her in his drunken parties, excesses and wantonness with other women.

—Plutarch

A woman we love rarely satisfies all our needs, and we deceive her with a woman whom we do not love.

—Marcel Proust

I think women force men to be unfaithful. Men are unfaithful by nature occasionally, but not as constantly as I was.

—Anthony Quinn

A man's heart may have a secret sanctuary where only one woman may enter, but it is full of little anterooms which are seldom vacant.

—Helen Rowland

I lost a girlfriend because I had to work so much. My wife is kind of happy about it, though.

—Ray Stevens

A lady temperance candidate concluded her passionate oration: "I would rather commit adultery than take a glass of beer." Whereupon a clear voice from the audience asked, "Who wouldn't?"

—Adlai Stevenson

Mistresses and wives are as different as night and day.

—Abigail Van Buren

Honesty has ruined more marriages than infidelity.

—Jimmy Williams

Insults

Fuck Grace Slick? I wouldn't even let her blow me.

—Marty Balin

Cher . . . has had so much cosmetic surgery that, for ease of maintenance, many of her body parts are attached with Velcro.

—Dave Barry

Mick Jagger is about as sexy as a pissing toad.

—Truman Capote

I said I didn't think Chevy Chase could ad-lib and fart after a baked bean dinner.

—Johnny Carson

Be a little more magnanimous and a little less of a cunt.

—Cher on Madonna

You're a boring fuck.

—Joan Collins to Arthur Loew
when he accused her of being
a "fucking bore"

Richard, I do believe you would screw a snake if you had the chance.

—Joan Collins to Richard Burton

Joan Crawford—Hollywood's first case of syphilis. I wouldn't sit on her toilet.

—Bette Davis

Slept with every male star at MGM except Lassie.

—Bette Davis on Joan Crawford

Dramatic in her opinion is knowing how to fill a sweater.

—Bette Davis on Jayne Mansfield

The mother-in-law thinks I'm effeminate; not that I mind because, beside her, I am.

—Les Dawson

I acted vulgar. Madonna is vulgar.

—Marlene Dietrich

They don't have a page that broad.

—Gennifer Flowers on Hillary Clinton appearing nude in a men's magazine like she did

It must be tough having a beautiful mother like Cher and being named Chastity. I guess the only thing worse would be being beautiful and being named Slut.

—Ava Gardner

Sleeping with George Michael would be like having sex with a groundhog.

—Boy George

Phallocentric someone once said of Freud. He thought the sun revolved around the penis.

—Erica Jong

Michael Jackson is the polar opposite of President Clinton, in many respects. Michael Jackson is constantly, constantly, desperately trying to make us believe he's having sex with women.

—David Letterman

I would say, "You are a butthead."

—Barbara Lewinsky on what she would say to Bill Clinton

If Clark had an inch less, he'd be the queen of Hollywood instead of the king.

—Carole Lombard on husband Clark Gable

God knows I love Clark, but he's the worst lay in town.

—Carole Lombard

He fucked every two-bit twat in Hollywood.

—Gary Marrill on Howard Hughes

The woman's disgusting. She called me a cunt. I'll never speak to her again.

—Bette Midler on Cher

She is so hairy—when she lifted up her arm, I thought it was Tina Turner in her armpit.

—Joan Rivers on Madonna

She's so pure, Moses couldn't even part her knees.

—Joan Rivers on Marie Osmond

While I was very fond of Paul Newman and Peter Sellers, I'd have to say I would rather kiss a tree trunk.

—Elke Sommer, wife of Sellers

I would have sex with sand before I'd have sex with Roseanne.

—Howard Stern

In five years you'll be dried up like a piece of shit in the desert. You'll look like a Tootsie Roll.

—Howard Stern on Sharon Stone

And you can actually have nasal sex with her. Triple penetration: oral, anal, and nasal.

—Matt Zone on Barbra Streisand

Jealousy

The jealousy of the harlot is evidenced by adultery, that of the virtuous woman by weeping.

—Egyptian proverb

A woman without jealousy is like a ball without bounce.

—English proverb

I think the only jealousy worth having is sexual jealousy. If I find something out, I go. I'm not a masochist. I don't hang around.

—Jean Marsh

To jealousy, nothing is more frightful than laughter.

—Françoise Sagan

Kinky Behavior

The biggest misconception about me is that I'm sleeping with my daughter.

—Woody Allen

An old pedophile . . . There's this incredibly twisted, sordid relationship.

—Mia Farrow on Woody Allen's
relationship with Soon-Yi, the
adopted daughter of Mia, the
mother of his children

Everyone knows not to have an affair with your son's sister.

—Moses Previn, fifteen, in a letter
to Woody Allen

He was the kind of guy who could kiss you behind your ear and make you feel like you'd just had kinky sex.

—Julia Alvarez on a boyfriend

When a masochist brings someone home and puts the moves on her, does he say, "Excuse me a moment, I'm going to slip into something uncomfortable?"

—George Carlin

I hear in Canada you only have sex doggy style; that way you can both see the hockey game.

—Rodney Dangerfield

It is very disturbing indeed when you can't think of any new perversions that you would like to practice.

—James Dickey

Comedy, like sodomy, is an unnatural act.

—Marty Feldman

Billy Idol would get so fucked up and high, he'd want girls to shove everything in sight up his butt.

—Heidi Fleiss

Of all sexual aberrations, chastity is the strangest.

—Anatole France

A pretty foot is one of the greatest gifts of nature . . . Please send me your last pair of shoes, already worn out in dancing, so I can have something of yours to press against my heart.

—Johann Wolfgang von Goethe

Call it incest, but I want my mommy.

—Graffito

Kinky is using a feather. Perverted is using the whole chicken.

—Graffito

Buttock fetishism is comparatively rare in our culture. Girls are often self-conscious about their behinds . . . Often because they are too abundant in that region than otherwise.

—Germaine Greer

Coffee without caffeine is like sex without the spanking.

—Trevor Cupid Hale

He kissed the plump mellow yellor smellor melons of her rump, on each plump melonous hemisphere, in their mellow yellow furrow, with obscure prolonged provocative melonsmellonous osculation.

—James Joyce

Most of our sexuality delinquent behavior is a direct result of sex being such a taboo subject, such an unspeakable thing.

—Madonna

He's into fun and games in bed, all the really horny things I get off on, like spanking, handcuffs, whips and Polaroid pictures.

—Karen Mayo-Chandler on
Jack Nicholson

I could have made a fortune as a dominatrix.

—Camille Paglia

A Greek is somebody who gets a little behind in his work.

—Bruce Rodgers

It was one of those bachelor parties where all the married men had to meet at the end and decide about what to say we did. "We got in a fight with some guys and that's how our underwear got ripped. They ripped our underwear, and smelled good. Jimmy, you fell and your nipple got pierced."

—Ray Romano

. . . using drumsticks very gently. It was just tapping on her private parts down there, where it's most sensitive, just using the tip of it on the private part there. And it was effective.

—Tiny Tim on love-making with
his wife, Miss Vicky

I'm all for bringing back the birch, but only between consenting adults.

—Gore Vidal

The only thing better than sex is sex with chocolate on top.

—Catherine Zeta-Jones

Kissing

Never let a fool kiss you or a kiss fool you.

—Joey Adams

A kiss is a lovely trick designed by nature to stop speech when words become superfluous.

—Ingrid Bergman

You must not kiss and tell.

—William Congreve

Any man who can drive safely while kissing a pretty girl is simply not giving the kiss the attention it deserves.

—Albert Einstein

One special form of contact, which consists of mutual approximation of the mucous membranes of the lips in a kiss, has received a sexual value among the civilized nations, though the parts of the body do not belong to the sexual apparatus and merely form the entrance to the digestive tract.

—Sigmund Freud

A kiss must last long to be enjoyed.

—Greek proverb

The sound of a kiss is not so loud as that of a cannon, but its echo lasts a great deal longer.

—Oliver Wendell Holmes

A kiss can be a comma, a question mark or an exclamation point.

—Mistinguett

A man snatches the first kiss, pleads for the second, demands the third, takes the fourth, accepts the fifth—and endures all the rest.

—Helen Rowland

To a woman the first kiss is just the end of the beginning, but to a man it is the beginning of the end.

—Helen Rowland

Lord! I wonder what fool it was that first invented kissing.

—Jonathan Swift

A man's kiss is his signature.

—Mae West

I've kissed so many women I can do it with my eyes closed.

—Henny Youngman

Love

Everyone admits that love is wonderful and necessary, yet no one can agree on what it is.

—Diane Ackerman

Falling in love is so hard on the knees.

—Aerosmith

The price of shallow sex may be a corresponding loss of capacity for deep love.

—Shana Alexander

Sex without love is an empty experience, but as empty experiences go, it's one of the best.

—Woody Allen

In real love you want the other person's good. In romantic love you want the other person.

—Margaret Anderson

Nobody dies from lack of sex. It's lack of love we die from.

—Margaret Atwood

Better to have loved and lost, than to have never loved at all.

—St. Augustine

Nuptial love maketh mankind; friendly love perfecteth it; but wanton love corrupteth and embaseth it.

—Francis Bacon

What the world really needs is more love and less paperwork.

—Pearl Bailey

Love is like a card trick. After you know how it works, it's no fun anymore.

—Fanny Brice

When love is out of your life, you're through in a way. Because while it is there it's like a motor that's going, you have such vitality to do things, big things, because love is goosing you all the time.

—Fanny Brice

Everything we do in life is based on fear, especially love.

—Mel Brooks

When success comes in the door, it seems, love often goes out the window.

—Dr. Joyce Brothers

A narcissism shared by two.

—Rita Mae Brown

All policy's allowed in war and love.

—Susannah Centlivre

Falling madly in love with someone is not necessarily the starting point to get married.

—Prince Charles

Free love is too expensive.

—Bernadette Devlin

Gravitation is not responsible for people falling in love.

—Albert Einstein

All mankind loves a lover.

—Ralph Waldo Emerson

I don't want to live—I want to love first, and live incidentally.

—Zelda Fitzgerald

He who falls in love with himself will have no rivals.
—Benjamin Franklin

He who marries for love has good nights and bad days.
—French proverb

Where they love they do not desire and where they desire they do not love.
—Sigmund Freud

Immature love says: I love you because I need you. Mature love says: I need you because I love you.
—Erich Fromm

Love is the irresistible desire to be irresistibly desired.
—Robert Frost

Love is a metaphysical gravity.
—R. Buckminster Fuller

I always say a girl must get married for love—and keep on getting married until she finds it.
—Zsa Zsa Gabor

Because it corresponds to a vital need, love is overvalued in our culture. It becomes a phantom—like success—carrying with it the illusion that it is a solution for all problems.
—Karen Horney

Love doesn't make the world go around. Love is what makes the ride worthwhile.
—Franklin P. Jones

If you want to read about love and marriage, you've got to buy two separate books.
—Alan King

Romantic love is mental illness. But it's a pleasurable one. It's a drug. It distorts reality, and that's the point of it. It would be impossible to fall in love with someone that you really saw.

—Fran Lebowitz

It requires infinitely greater genius to make love, than to make war.

—Ninon de Lenclos

Love lay like a mirage through the golden gates of sex.

—Doris Lessing

Love is what happens to men and women who don't know each other.

—W. Somerset Maugham

Early love, chemically based, is when you love the way the other person makes you feel. It is self-centered, feel-good love. Mature love, which comes later in a relationship, is love for whoever a person is. It is other-centered.

—Charles Panati

Love is like quicksilver in the hand. Leave the finger open and it stays. Clutch it, and it darts away.

—Dorothy Parker

The greatest love is motherlove; after that comes a dog's love; after that the love of a sweetheart.

—Polish proverb

It is one's own personal, selfish happiness that one seeks, earns, and derives from love.

—Ayn Rand

Never forget that the most powerful force on earth is love.

—Nelson Rockefeller

It is better to have loved your wife than never to have loved at all.

—Edgar Saltus

Love is merely a madness.

—William Shakespeare

Love is the only disease that makes you feel better.

—Sam Shepard

A wise woman will marry the man who loves her rather than the one she loves.

—Slovenian proverb

Is there any greater or keener pleasure than that of sexual love?

—Socrates

Sex without love is as hollow and ridiculous as love without sex.

—Hunter S. Thompson

Love is much nicer to be in than an automobile accident, a tight girdle, a higher tax bracket, or a holding pattern over Philadelphia.

—Judith Viorst

We love as soon as we learn to distinguish a separate "you" and "me." Love is our attempt to assuage the terror and isolation of that separateness.

—Judith Viorst

Love is the same as like except you feel sexier.
—Judith Viorst

Sex with love is the greatest thing in life. But sex without love—that's not so bad either.
—Mae West

If love is blind, why is lingerie so popular?
—Jimmy Williams

Machismo

What's with you men? Would hair stop growing on your chest if you asked directions somewhere?
—Erma Bombeck

A man needs the sexual conquest to prove that he can still do it, that he can still get it up . . . He has to prove it all the time.
—Princess Elizabeth of Yugoslavia

American men are all mixed up today . . . There was a time when this was a nation of Ernest Hemingways, real men. The kind of men who could defoliate an entire forest to make a breakfast fire—and then wipe out an endangered species while hunting for lunch. But not any more . . . We've become a nation of wimps. Pansies. Alan Alda types who cook and clean and "relate" to their wives. Phil Donahue clones who are "sensitive" and "vulnerable" and understanding of their children. And where's it gotten us? I'll tell you where. The Japanese make better cars. The Israelis better soldiers. And the rest of the world is using our embassies for target practice.
—Bruce Feirstein

The tragedy of machismo is that a man is never quite man enough.

—Germaine Greer

I grew up around macho men and had lovers that are that macho type. I'm kinda drawn to that for my lovers for the most part.

—Dolly Parton

Testosterone does not have to be toxic.

—Anna Quindlen

Men may deny it, but I think they're motivated to succeed to be incredibly powerful and opulent and to maintain an overwhelming, titanic status in the community for women. It is a sexual thing—it's done for either hands-on sexual gratification or for sexual allure. Power. That's what women are drawn to.

—Sylvester Stallone

A confirmed bachelor is a guy who believes in wine, women, and so long.

—John Travolta

Male Chauvinism

People ask me how many children I have and I say one boy and seven mistakes.

—Muhammad Ali

The male is by nature superior, and the female inferior; and the one rules, and the other ruled, of necessity, extends to all mankind . . . The lower sort are by nature slaves, and it is better for them as for all inferiors that they should be under the rule of a master.

—Aristotle

You know why God invented woman? Because sheep can't type.

—Kenneth Armbrister

There are only three things that women are better at than men: cleaning, cooking and having sex.

—Charles Barkley

No one is more arrogant toward women, more aggressive or scornful, than the man who is anxious about his virility.

—Simone de Beauvoir

The only thing that holds a marriage together is the husband being big enough to step back and see where his wife is wrong.

—Archie Bunker

A woman is but an animal, and an animal not of the highest order.

—Edmund Burke

I like women to move when I'm on top of them.

—Hugh Cornwell on the
women's movement

Marriage is very difficult. Very few of us are fortunate enough to marry multimillionaire girls with thirty-nine inch busts who have undergone frontal lobotomies.

—Tony Curtis

There's nothing tougher than remembering why you've chased a dame once you've had her.

—Clint Eastwood

Why did I call this chapter "Leave it to Beaver"? Because that's what some of the men at NBC News called *Overnight*. The first network news program run by women.

—Linda Ellerbee

The fear of sexual assault is a special fear: its intensity in women can best be likened to the male fear of castration.

—Germaine Greer

Isn't she the most beautiful maid you've ever seen in your life?

—Don Johnson on wife
Melanie Griffith

There's only two things you people are good for: having babies and frying bacon.

—Bobby Knight to a female
reporter

Look, Mr. President, I might sleep with them, but I'm damned if I'll eat lunch with them.

—Bill Lawrence to John F.
Kennedy on admitting women
to an all-male club

Girls begin to talk and to stand on their feet sooner than boys because weeds always grow up more quickly than good crops.

—Martin Luther

A woman's place is in the bedroom.

—Ferdinand Marcos

Nature intended women to be our slaves . . . They are our property, we are not theirs . . . They belong to us, just as a tree which bears fruit belongs to the gardener. What a mad idea to demand equality for women! Women are nothing but machines for producing children.

—Napoleon

There's nothing so similar to one poodle dog as another poodle dog, and that goes for women too.

—Pablo Picasso

Of those who were born as men, all that were cowardly and spent their life in wrongdoing were transformed at the second birth into women . . . Such is the origin of women and of all that is female.

—Plato

A woman always wants to be dominated in bed, but is afraid to admit it. A woman is good in bed if she accepts the fact that she is going to be fucked . . . a willing slave is always warm and humble and submissive and happy to be a slave.

—Oliver Reed

I know it's a sexist opinion, but I hold it nonetheless: women do not park as well as men.

—Andy Rooney

Women are great. When they dig you, there's nothing they won't do. That kind of loyalty is hard to find—unless you've got a good dog.

—David Lee Roth

It is naive in the extreme for women to be regarded as equals by men so long as they persist in subhuman (i.e. animal-like) behavior during sexual intercourse; I'm referring to the outlandish PANTING, GASPING, MOANING, SOBBING, WRITHING, SCRATCHING, BITING, SCREAMING, and the seemingly invariable OH MY GOD . . . All so predictably integral to pre-, post-, and orgasmic stages of intercourse.

—Terry Southern

I don't know what kind of doctor I am. But watching all these beautiful sisters here . . . I'm debating whether I should be a gynecologist.

—Mike Tyson when receiving an honorary doctorate degree

There are three intolerable things in life—cold coffee, lukewarm champagne, and overexcited women.

—Orson Welles

Marriage

I prefer the word "homemaker" because "housewife" always implies that there may be a wife someplace else.

—Bella Abzug

If it were not for the presents, an elopement would be preferable.

—George Ade

He who marries a beauty marries trouble.

—African proverb

Happiness in marriage is entirely a matter of chance.

—Jane Austen

The majority of husbands remind me of an orangutan trying to play the violin.

—Honoré de Balzac

No man should marry until he has studied anatomy and dissected at least one woman.

—Honoré de Balzac

It isn't premarital sex if you have no intention of getting married.

—Matt Barry

The husband who doesn't tell his wife everything probably reasons that what she doesn't know won't hurt him.

—Leo J. Burke

Before getting married, find out if you're really in love— ask yourself, "Would I mind getting financially destroyed by this person?"

—Johnny Carson

If variety is the spice of life, marriage is the big can of leftover Spam.

—Johnny Carson

Thank God for single people. America would never have been found if Christopher Columbus had been married; "You're going where? With whom? To find what? And I suppose she's giving you those ships for nothing?"

—Richard Chamberlain

If you are afraid of loneliness, don't marry.

—Anton Chekhov

He who marries might be sorry; he who does not will be sorry.

—Czech proverb

Marriage is to courting as humming is to singing.

—Peter De Vries

That's like letting a wife come between friendships. Friends are hard to find; you can find a wife anywhere.

—Mike Ditka

Marriage probably originated as a straightforward food-for-sex deal among foraging primates. Compatibility was not a big issue, nor, of course, was there any tension over who would control the remote.

—Barbara Ehrenreich

I would rather be a beggar and single, than a Queen and married . . . I should call the wedding ring the yoke ring.

—Queen Elizabeth I

It seemed to me that the desire to get married, which I regret to say I believe is basic and primal in women, is followed almost immediately by an equal basic and primal urge—which is to be single again.

—Nora Ephron

No, it just seems longer.

—W. C. Fields on whether
married people live longer

I don't think it's natural for two people to swear to be together for the rest of their lives.

—Jane Fonda

They're saying that my ability to marry another man somehow jeopardizes heterosexual marriage. Then they go out and cheat on their wives. That doesn't jeopardize heterosexual marriage?

—Barney Frank

One good husband is worth two good wives; for the scarcer things are the more they're valued.

—Benjamin Franklin

Maybe I got married a few too many times. It's because I love a good party, but I have recently realized that I can actually just throw a party and not get married.

—Whoopi Goldberg

A great marriage is the union of two forgivers.

—Ruth Bell Graham

I've been married to one Marxist and one Fascist and neither one would take the garbage out.

—Lee Grant

After marriage, all things change. And one of them better be you.

—Elizabeth Hawes

If you want to sacrifice the admiration of many men for the criticism of one, go ahead and get married.

—Katharine Houghton Hepburn
to daughter Katharine

I have learned that only two things are necessary to keep one's wife happy. First, let her think she's having her own way. Second, let her have it.

—Lyndon Baines Johnson

I never knew what real happiness was until I got married. And then it was too late.

—Max Kauffmann

I'd like to get married again, but I'm afraid of that marital commitment—we're talking two, three years of my life.

—Laura Kennedy

Sex when you're married is like going to the 7-Eleven—there's not much variety, but at three in the morning, it's always there.

—Carol Leifer

I have now come to the conclusion never again to think of marrying, and for this reason: I can never be satisfied with anyone who would be blockhead enough to have me.

—Abraham Lincoln

Women do generally manage to love the guys they marry more than they manage to marry the guys they love.

—Clare Boothe Luce

It is ridiculous to think you can spend your entire life with just one person. Three is about the right number. Yes, I imagine three husbands would do it.

—Clare Boothe Luce

The husband who wants a happy marriage should learn to keep his mouth shut and his checkbook open.

—Groucho Marx

A man marries to have a home, but also because he doesn't want to be bothered with sex and all that sort of thing.

—W. Somerset Maugham

A successful marriage requires falling in love many times, always with the same person.

—Mignon McLaughlin

It's not that marriage itself is bad; it's the people we marry who give it a bad name.

—Terry McMillan

A man may be a fool and not know it, but not if he's married.

—H. L. Mencken

Marriage is far and away the most sanitary and least harmful of all the impossible forms of the man-woman relationship, though I would sooner jump off the Brooklyn bridge than be married.

—H. L. Mencken

Before marriage, a girl has to make love to a man to hold him. After marriage, she has to hold him to make love to him.

—Marilyn Monroe

A great marriage is not so much finding the right person as being the right person.

—Marabel Morgan

The law has made the man and wife one person, and that one person the husband.

—Lucretia Mott

He tells you when you've got too much lipstick, and helps you with your girdle when your hips stick.

—Ogden Nash on husbands

With children no longer the universally accepted reason for marriage, marriages are going to have to exist on their own merits.

—Eleanor Holmes Norton

Were marriage no more than a convenient screen for sexuality, some less cumbersome and costly protection must have been found by this time to replace it. One concludes therefore that people do not marry to cohabitate; they cohabitate to marry.

—Virgilia Peterson

When a man opens a car door for his wife, it's either a new car or a new wife.

—Prince Philip

I believe in the institution of marriage and I intend to keep trying until I get it right.

—Richard Pryor

Alas, why will a man spend months trying to hand over his liberty to a woman—and the rest of his life trying to get it back again?

—Helen Rowland

Marriage is a souvenir of love.

—Helen Rowland

Marriage is like twirling a baton, turning a handspring or eating with chopsticks; it looks so easy until you try it.

—Helen Rowland

Before marriage, a man will go home and lie awake all night thinking about something you said; after marriage, he'll go to sleep before you finish saying it.

—Helen Rowland

I love being married. It's so great to find that one special person you want to annoy for the rest of your life.

—Rita Rudner

Men who have a pierced ear are better prepared for marriage. They've experienced pain and bought jewelry.

—Rita Rudner

In Hollywood a marriage is a success if it outlasts the milk.

—Rita Rudner

I'd like to talk about the sex I have with my wife, but when you're married you're not supposed to say, "Hey, I did my wife last night." It's okay if you're in a bar and say, "See that chick over there? I did her." People go, "All right. Good for you." But if it's your wife, they don't want to hear about it and you aren't supposed to talk about it.

—Bob Sagat

There is so little difference between husbands, you might as well keep the first.

—Adela Rogers St. John

I began as a passion and ended as a habit, like all husbands.

—George Bernard Shaw

Marriage is an alliance entered into by a man who can't sleep with the window shut, and a woman who can't sleep with the window open.

—George Bernard Shaw

Marriage is not a man's idea. A woman must have thought of it. Years ago some guy said, "Let me get this straight, honey. I can't sleep with anyone else for the rest of my life, and if things don't work out, you get to keep half my stuff? What a great idea."

—Bobby Slayton

He who can't do any better goes to bed with his own wife.

—Spanish proverb

. . . no woman should marry a teetotaller, or a man who does not smoke.

—Robert Lewis Stevenson

While I was ironing one evening, it suddenly occurred to me that I, too, would like to have a wife . . . My God, who wouldn't want a wife?

—Judy Syfers

What do you expect me to do? Sleep alone?

—Elizabeth Taylor on her many marriages

. . . marriage cannot cause happiness. Instead, it is always torture, which man has to pay for satisfying his sex urge.

—Leo Tolstoy

One advantage of marriage is that when you fall out of love with him or he falls out of love with you, it keeps you together until you fall in love again.

—Judith Viorst

Honey, I'm single because I was born that way. I never married, because I would have had to give up my favorite hobby—men.

—Mae West

Men marry because they are tired; women, because they are curious. Both are disappointed.

—Oscar Wilde

Niagara Falls is only the second biggest disappointment of the standard honeymoon.

—Oscar Wilde

The most difficult years of any marriage are those after the wedding.

—Jimmy Williams

No chupa, no shtupa—no wedding, no bedding.

—Yiddish proverb

The secret of a happy marriage remains a secret.

—Henny Youngman

Masturbation

When the habit is discovered, it must in young children be put to a stop by such means as tying the hands, strapping the knees together with a pad between them.

—Ada Ballin

You are throwing away the seed that has been handed down to you as a trust instead of keeping it and ripening it for bringing a son to you later.

—Lord Baden-Powell, founder of
the Boy Scouts, advising the
troops

I'll come and make love to you at five o'clock. If I'm late, start without me.

—Tallulah Bankhead

Interference with self-pleasure is a very bad thing for children.

—Mary Calderone

If God intended us not to masturbate, He would have made our arms shorter.

—George Carlin

If you have sex and you know you've made the other person happy, it's so much better than doing it for yourself. Although if you're using your left hand, it's really like you're with someone else.

—Jim Carrey

Marilyn Monroe was a masturbation fantasy of bellboys; Grace Kelly of bank executives.

—James Dickey

As per your specific question in regards to masturbation, I think that is something that is part of human sexuality and it's a part of something that perhaps should be taught [in public schools].

—Joycelyn Elders

We weren't talking about teaching the how-to. We were just talking about teaching against the lies, that self-stimulation won't cause you harm.

—Joycelyn Elders defending her theory

We were poor. If I wasn't a boy, I wouldn't have had nothing to play with.

—Redd Foxx

Never pull off tomorrow what you can pull off today.

—Graffito

Masturbation is the thinking man's television.

—Christopher Hampton

Masturbation is the thief of love.

—Tim and Beverly LaHaye

Playing with oneself (eighteenth-twentieth c.) is a worthwhile activity for both sexes and one of the most rewarding of all the sexual practices. In terms of orgasmic efficacy, it seldom fails us. Alfred Kinsey reported that 95 percent of the time it is successful, with 75 percent of the participants attaining climax (twentieth c.) in less than four minutes.

—Lawrence Paros

Intercourse counterfeits masturbation.

—Jean-Paul Sartre

Masturbation is the primary sexual activity of mankind. In the nineteenth century it was a disease; in the twentieth, it's a cure.

—Thomas Szasz

114

We have reason to believe that man first walked upright to free his hands for masturbation.

—Lily Tomlin

If sex is so personal, why are we expected to share it with someone else?

—Lily Tomlin

Of all the various kinds of sexual intercourse this has the least to recommend it. As an amusement it is too fleeting. As an occupation it is too wearing. As a public exhibition there is no money in it. It is unsuited to the drawing room.

—Mark Twain

I'm not weird or anything. I don't tie myself up first.

—Tom Waits

Good sex is like playing bridge. If you don't have a good partner, you'd better have a good hand.

—Mae West

When jacking off is outlawed, only outlaws will jack off.

—Jimmy Williams

Secretary of Education Joycelyn Elders resigned because of opposition to her plans to make masturbation a high school course. Damn, just when there's something I can finally teach. I could write the manual. It's a hands-on course. And it has a great final exam.

—Robin Williams

Men

I am more and more convinced that man is a dangerous creature.

—Abigail Adams

About sex especially men are born unbalanced; we might say men are born mad. They scarcely reach sanity till they reach sanctity.

—G. K. Chesterton

However much men say sex is not on their minds all the time, it is—most of the time.

—Jackie Collins

The compulsion to find a lover and husband in a single person has doomed more women to misery than any other illusion.

—Carolyn Heilbrun

A man's home may seem to be his castle on the outside; inside it is more often his nursery.

—Clare Boothe Luce

Women are taking the man out of their men, and I don't like that. A woman needs a man whom she can't control.

—Loretta Lynn

There is nothing about which men lie so much as their sexual powers. In this at least every man is, what in his heart he would like to be, a Casanova.

—W. Somerset Maugham

Man's role is uncertain, undefined, and perhaps unnecessary.

—Margaret Mead

Don't accept rides from strange men, and remember that all men are strange as hell.

—Robin Morgan

There are men I could spend eternity with. But not in this life.

—Kathleen Norris

Behind every successful man is a surprised wife.

—Maryon Pearson

I like the concept of "men." It's the reality I have trouble with.

—Stephanie H. Piro

Men would always rather be made love to than talked at.

—Dorothy M. Richardson

The more I see of men, the more I like dogs.

—Madame de Staël

Every man I meet wants to protect me. I can't figure out what from.

—Mae West

A man is by nature a sexual animal. I've always had my special pets.

—Mae West

A man in the house is worth two in the street.

—Mae West

I don't love women the way I love men. I love men pretty much. They're interesting. I'm more tolerant of them. I can say, "Oh, he's an asshole, but I love him." But if she's an asshole, she's an asshole.

—Debra Winger

Money

The most popular labor-saving device today is still a husband with money.

—Joey Adams

Money can't buy love—but it certainly puts you into a wonderful bargaining position.

—Harrison Baker

Money, it turned out, was exactly like sex; you thought of nothing else if you didn't have it and of other things if you did.

—James Baldwin

I'm a quadrasexual. That means I'll do anything with anyone for a quarter.

—Ed Bluestone

My only aversion to vice,
Is the price.

—Victor Buono

There is no economy in going to bed early to save electricity if the result be twins.

—Chinese proverb

Even if you studied history or zoology or physics and hoped to spend your life pursuing some difficult and challenging career, you still had a mind full of all the soupy longings that every high school girl was awash in . . . Underneath it all you longed to be annihilated by love, to be filled up by a giant prick sprouting sperm, soapsuds, silks and satins, and, of course, money.

—Erica Jong

It costs a lot of money to look this cheap.

—Dolly Parton

When you are in love with someone you want to be near him all the time, except when you are out buying things and charging them to him.

—Miss Piggy

Part of the loot went for gambling, part for horses, and part for women. The rest I spent foolishly.

—George Raft on spending his considerable earnings

I spend mine [money] on shit I couldn't afford: a car, not paying taxes. My whole life at the time was trying to fuck girls I had no business fucking.

—Chris Rock

Were it not for gold and women, there would be no damnation.

—Cyril Tourneur

Sex is like money, golf and beer—even when it's bad, it's good.

—Jimmy Williams

Monogamy

Polygamy is dumb fun.

—Warren Beatty

I didn't get married under the premise or the deceit that my ex-husband was anything closely resembling monogamous . . . So I cultivated and knew and was very friendly with the groupies that were involved.

—Angie Bowie, David's ex-wife

Monogamy is contrary to nature but necessary for the greater social good.

—Rita Mae Brown

Lifelong monogamy is a maniacal idea.

—Germaine Greer

Hogamus, higamus
Man is polygamous
Higamus, hogamus
Woman monogamous

—William James

Bigamy is having one husband too many. Monogamy is the same.

—Erica Jong

Monogamous heterosexual love is probably one of the most difficult, complex and demanding of human relationships.

—Margaret Mead

Monogamy is monogamy until you screw someone else.

—River Phoenix

Even in civilized mankind faint traces of monogamous instinct can be perceived.

—Bertrand Russell

Monogamy is the Western custom of one wife and hardly any mistresses.

—Saki

I've never bought that open marriage thing. I've never seen it work. But that doesn't mean I believe in monogamy. Sleeping with someone else doesn't necessarily constitute infidelity.

—Carly Simon

Music

If I had to choose between music and sex, I would pause a long time.

—Donald Barthelme

Madam, you have between your legs an instrument capable of giving pleasure to thousands and all you can do is scratch it.

—Sir Thomas Beecham to a lady cellist

I would like to play for audiences who are not using my music to stimulate their sex organs.

—Ornette Coleman

The worst part of being gay in the twentieth century is all that damn disco music to which one has to listen.

—Quentin Crisp

Sex, drugs and rock and roll are why most people get into this business [music]. Most guys in the bands who have tons of sex, drugs and rock and roll weren't getting any in high school.

—Carson Daly

Most people get into bands for three very simple rock 'n' roll reasons: to get laid, to get fame, and to get rich.

—Bob Geldof

My favorite song title: "I Can't Get Over You Until You Get Out From Under Him."

—Lewis Grizzard

There are three kinds of pianists; Jewish pianists, homosexual pianists and bad pianists.

—Vladimir Horowitz

On stage, I make love to 25,000 different people, then I go home alone.

—Janis Joplin

I always thought music was more important than sex— then I thought if I don't hear a concert for a year-and-a-half it doesn't bother me.

—Jackie Mason

All my songs are about sex. Nashville likes to pretend it doesn't exist. They should loosen up. Everyone's doing it, aren't they?

—Mindy McCready

A lot of tunes in the guise of romanticism have mainly fucking behind them.

—Randy Newman

When you fuck a lot, you learn how a woman moves. When you play a lot, you learn how the audience moves.

—Ted Nugent

I love sex as much as I love music, and I think it's as hard to do.

—Linda Ronstadt

Classic Van Halen made you want to drink, dance, and fuck. Current Van Halen encourages us to drink milk, drive a Nissan, and have a relationship.

—David Lee Roth

I knew I could strap a guitar around my neck and have girls lick my boot heels.

—Gene Simmons

If you don't have any groupies hanging around, then obviously you're not really making it.

—Frank Zappa

Nudity

I'm quitting [the Olympic basketball team] for the swim team. I'm going to the pool as long as there are babes with no tops.

—Charles Barkley

When I first realized I was good looking, I was naked, looking at myself in the mirror. Then later, I got around to looking at my face.

—David Bowie

Strippers are generally open minded . . . Whatever you want, they'll say, "All right." Sex is so matter-of-fact with them.

—Drew Carey

According to a new survey, women say they feel more comfortable undressing in front of men than they do undressing in front of other women. They say that women are too judgmental, whereas, of course, men are just grateful.

—Robert De Niro

The best contraceptive for old people is nudity.

—Phyllis Diller

Never trust a naked bus driver.

—Jack Douglas

I hope I don't get a hard on—it would be distracting to the crew and I'd be embarrassed because, shit, maybe it's not as big as I want it to be.

—Robert Downey Jr. on doing a
nude scene

It's practically old-fashioned today to think of nudity in any other terms than normal.

—Jane Fonda

But at strip clubs I pay a ten-dollar cover, a beautiful nude woman dances inches away from my face, I can't touch her, she can't touch me, I can't touch myself, and I give her all my money. You know that's what hell has to be like.

—Jeff Garlin

I'm wise enough to know what I didn't know when I did my first nude scene: it's all commercial bananas and nothing to do with what is valuable to the script.

—Susan Hampshire

I'll tell you what: if you become our Playmate for July, I'll get you that new addressograph for your department.

—Hugh Hefner to Charlaine
Karalus, *Playboy* subscription
manager, who got the machine

Nowadays, when the models open and display their sex, they look straight into the sucker's eyes, just the way a grocer does when he assures his customer the mango is ripe.

—Irma Kurta

When Sophia Loren is naked, this is a lot of nakedness.

—Sophia Loren

One of my correspondents has me convinced that the human race would be saved if the world became a nudist colony. I keep thinking how much harder it would be to carry concealed weapons.

—Cyra McFadden

I'm just looking for that moment to drop my Jedi knickers and pull out my real light saber.

—Ewan McGregor

I had the radio on.

—Marilyn Monroe when asked if
she really had nothing on in a
calendar photograph

I am only comfortable when I'm naked.

—Marilyn Monroe

It's about time that people forget that image of strip clubs as seedy places . . . Rather, today's strip clubs are capital-intensive female-empowerment zones.

—Demi Moore

There are certain people who should know what you look like naked. I just don't think your high school algebra teacher is one of them.

—Julia Roberts on appearing
naked in a film

Acting is standing up naked and turning around very slowly.

—Rosalind Russell

I've done a couple of sex scenes, and they're not much fun. You're in a room with lots of people, trying to pretend you're alone and you're naked. I've never met an actor who says, "Let's have some fun and do some love scenes."

—Ben Stiller

We don't see that many of our male stars' frontal nudity. It makes me uncomfortable to be in an unequal position.

—Meryl Streep on why she
doesn't do nude scenes

Many people may be depressed by the spectacle of naked humanity. Personally I can't see that an ugly body is any more offensive than an ugly dress.

—Evelyn Waugh

Observations and Opinions

You're not supposed to mention fucking in mixed company, and yet that's precisely the place you're supposed to do it.

—George Carlin

Life is like a beautiful flirt, whom we love and to whom, finally, we grant every condition she imposes as long as she doesn't leave us.

—Casanova

We've surrounded the most vital and commonplace human function with a vast morass of taboos, conventions, hypocrisy, and plain claptrap.

—Ilka Chase

Nothing in our culture, not even home computers, is more overrated than the epidermal felicity of two featherless bipeds in desperate congress.

—Quentin Crisp

In Spain lust is in the air. There is nothing clandestine about the Spanish appreciation of sex, nothing inhibited or restrained. That is why there are very few sexual crimes in Spain.

—Fernando Diaz-Plaja

You see an awful lot of smart guys with dumb women, but you hardly ever see a smart woman with a dumb guy.

—Clint Eastwood

Sex can be overrated.

—Clint Eastwood

Sometimes a cigar is just a cigar.

—Sigmund Freud

Sexuality is the great battle between biology and society.

—Nancy Friday

Sex and laughter do go very well together, and I wondered—and still do—which is the more important.

—Hermione Gingold

You must just acknowledge deep in your heart of hearts that people are supposed to fuck. It is the main purpose in life; all those other activities—playing the trumpet, vacuuming carpets, reading mystery novels, eating chocolate mousse—are just ways of passing time until you can fuck again.

—Cynthia Heimel

An intellectual is a person who's found one thing that's more interesting than sex.

—Aldous Huxley

Of all the things that human beings did together, the sexual act was the one with the most various of reasons.

—P. D. James

Sexual intercourse is like having someone else blow your nose.

—Philip Larkin

Sex, unlike justice, should not be seen to be done.

—Evelyn Laye

Penetration is good.

—Pamela Anderson Lee

People talk about "sex" as though it hopped about by itself, like a frog!

—Anne Morrow Lindbergh

It's true that the French have a certain obsession with sex, but it's a particularly adult obsession. France is the thriftiest of all nations; to a Frenchman sex provides the most economical way to have fun.

—Anita Loos

Sex is the most fun you can have without smiling.

—Madonna

Making love, we are all more alike than we are when we are talking or acting.

—Mary McCarthy

Life without sex might be safer but it would be unbearably dull.

—H. L. Mencken

Puritanism—the haunting fear that someone, somewhere, may be happy.

—H. L. Mencken

Everyone lies about sex, more or less, to themselves if not to others, to others if not to themselves, exaggerating its importance or minimizing its pull.

—Daphne Merkin

I think that in the sexual act, as delightful as it can be, the very physical part of it is, yes, a hammering away. So it has a certain brutality.

—Louise Nevelson

Balling is one of the best things we do in life, but TV is still tied to a moral taboo about it.

—Carroll O'Connor

What people do behind closed doors is certainly not my concern unless I'm behind there with them.

—Dolly Parton

The back seat produced the sexual revolution.

—Jerry Rubin

Sex for sex's sake on the screen seems childish to me, but it's violence that really bothers me.

—Rosalind Russell

It provokes the desire, but it takes away the performance. Therefore much drink may be said to be an equivocator with lechery.

—William Shakespeare

Sex has become one of the most discussed subjects of modern times. The Victorians pretended it did not exist; the moderns pretend that nothing else exists.

—Bishop Fulton J. Sheen

Since time began nobody has been able to copulate while asleep. Even if it were possible it would be impolite.

—Alan Sherman

In my view, a woman's sexuality cannot be separated from her whole personality. It's impossible to consider woman in isolation from man and the world we share. It seems to me that what happens in the vagina has more to do, in 1984, with H-Bombs than with G-spots.

—D. M. Thomas

Sex is a game, a weapon, a toy, a joy, a trance, an enlightenment, a loss, a hope.

—Sallie Tisdale

After being alive, the next hardest work is sex . . . Some people get energy from sex, and some people lose energy from sex. I have found that it's too much work.

—Andy Warhol

Sex is the biggest nothing of all time.

—Andy Warhol

When Madonna grabs her crotch, the social order is effectively transgressed.

—Chip Wells

An ounce of performance is worth pounds of promise.

—Mae West

It is something big and cosmic. What else do we have? There's only birth and death and the union of two people—and sex is the only one that happens to us more than once.

—Kathleen Winsor

On Others

I don't think he has changed that much. He still eyes a pretty lady—and why not? This is part of his magnetism. This is Warren. What has changed, I hope, is that he doesn't seem to have that urge to bed these lovely ladies. Now that is a major change.

—Annette Bening on husband
Warren Beatty

I've got to don my breast plate once more to play opposite Miss Tits.

—Richard Burton on Elizabeth
Taylor

I'm not easily shocked, but Patsy [Cline] got to me one time. We were working in Canada and checking into a hotel. She looked around the lobby and saw this big Canadian Mountie. Right out loud she snapped, "He's a big good-looking son of a bitch. I want him! I'm screwing the boots off him tonight." And she took off across to him and did what she said she was going to do.

—Jimmy Dean

He could handle women as smoothly as operating an elevator. He knew exactly where to locate the top button.

—Britt Ekland on Warren Beatty

I don't care if he boned a sheep, if that's his thing.

—Whoopi Goldberg on
Bill Clinton

He's different and doesn't talk, fuck, fuck, fuck all the time.

—Jean Harlow on her husband

Hugh Grant is fantastic in bed. He always has been.

—Elizabeth Hurley

. . . he slid his hand up my leg.

—Paula Jones on Bill Clinton

Shaking hands with Bill Clinton is in and of itself, a full body sexual experience, I promise you. He has the sexiest handshake of any man that I have ever experienced in my life.

—Judith Krantz

We haven't worked out all our problems, but the sex is better than ever.

—Pamela Anderson Lee on
reuniting with her husband

[Jimmy Carter] says his lust is in his heart. I hope it is a little lower.

—Shirley MacLaine

At dinner, Dustin Hoffman would occasionally fart while sitting at the table. When he farted, he'd waft it up to his face with his hands, then look at me and say, "It's my house." He can make me laugh so hard.

—John Malkovich

He's a perfectionist. If he was married to Raquel Welch, he'd expect her to cook.

—Don Meredith on coach
Tom Landry

I want to know how Bruce Willis fucks Demi Moore—in what position and how many times a week.

—Howard Stern

We elected him president, not pope.

—Barbra Streisand on
Bill Clinton

On Themselves

I want to be reincarnated as Warren Beatty's fingertips.
—Woody Allen

I resent the idea that you can't be sexy and smart. When I dyed my hair, the peroxide didn't fry my brain cells.
—Loni Anderson

I was an innocent sexually. [Humphrey Bogart] began awakening feelings that were new to me.
—Lauren Bacall

If I could go someplace like Norway and find a seventeen-year-old girl, I'd be a happy man. I'd train her.
—Corbin Bernsen

There is nothing wrong with my tits, but I don't go throwing them around in people's faces.
—Joan Crawford on
Marilyn Monroe

I can match bottoms with anyone in Hollywood.
—Mia Farrow

We're a bunch of hot-blooded babes with a lot of physical energy.
—Julie Foudy, co-captain of the
U.S. women's soccer team on
conjugal visits typically not
allowed by men's coaches

How can I forget the rainbow? I've got rainbows up my ass.
—Judy Garland

When I am married, I want to be single, and when I'm single, I want to be married.

—Cary Grant

I mean, if there were nothing but old whores and nasty, old, hard-looking women, I'd be out looking for some young, sweet, little fifteen-year-old boy.

—Don Johnson

I used to move in with people and fuck them because I thought they'd give me their powers. And they did.

—Courtney Love

Ah, wonderful women! Just give me a comfortable couch, a dog, a good book and a woman. Then if you can get the dog to go somewhere and read the book, I might have a little fun.

—Groucho Marx

I'm the white Anglo-Saxon male: I'm everybody's asshole. Black people think I'm physically deficient and oppressive, gay people think I'm latently homosexual and overly macho, women think I'm oafish and horny, and Asians think I'm lazy and stupid.

—Dennis Miller

It isn't the all-important thing for me to get a lay . . . If it's a matter of going to bed fine, but if it isn't, that's all right too. I appreciate women around like you would appreciate flowers. They add to the atmosphere.

—Henry Miller

We've never been a democracy; we've always been in a phallocracy.

—Françoise Parturier

Do we have sex? Yes, yes, yes.

—Lisa Marie Presley on her
marriage to Michael Jackson

I don't screw around. If I'd done one-third of what people say I have, if I'd had one-half the women, I'd be a
great man. But I haven't. I wish I had.

—Dan Rather

Edgar had a heart attack, and I'm to blame. We were
making love, and I took the bag off my head.

—Joan Rivers

I never believed in casual sex. I have always tried as
hard as I could.

—Garry Shandling

People ask me what I look for in women. I look for me
in women.

—Gene Simmons

I have a special butt. It has special curves, and it kind of
has its own attitude . . . I think the audience can feel
that, and if I were to try to put someone else's butt in
that place, the audience would feel cheated and emotionally insulted.

—Will Smith

I thought my usefulness was finished. After all, I believed my job on earth was to procreate and be a pleas-
ant sexual diversion for hard-working men.

—Margaret Trudeau on menopause

I thank God I was raised Catholic, so sex will always be
dirty.

—John Waters

When grown-ups do it, it's kind of dirty—that's because there's no one to punish them.

—Tuesday Weld

I'm never vulgar. I kid sex. I take it out in the open and laugh at it.

—Mae West

Oral Sex

I'd like to eat Mel Gibson literally and figuratively.

—Roseanne Barr

Clinton lied. A man might forget where he parks or where he lives, but he never forgets oral sex, no matter how bad it is.

—Barbara Bush

Making out is number one, eating pussy is number two . . . I love making a woman happy; eating pussy, shopping, whatever it takes.

—Drew Carey

I've just seen the tops of their heads.

—David Allan Coe on his groupies

No head, no backstage pass.

—David Allan Coe's road-crew T-Shirts

I've been sucked by the biggest names in Hollywood.

—James Dean

When I was younger I tried to go down on myself with some success. I actually could reach, and I remember thinking that was a big deal, but I couldn't do much down there.

—Whoopi Goldberg

I play the flute and swallow the music.

—Graffito

Think about him, talk about him, but don't go down for him.

—Graffito

Loves makes the world go down.

—Graffito

Oral sex is like being attacked by a giant snail.

—Germaine Greer

Even if you have only two seconds, drop everything and give him a blow job. That way, he won't really want sex with anyone else.

—Jerry Hall on how to keep your
man faithful

What I love doing most of all with a new lover is totally oral, that famous four-letter word ending with "k" that means intercourse which is, of course, talk.

—Xavier Hollander

The cure for starvation in India and the cure for over-population—both in one big swallow.

—Erica Jong

Start licking at the tip gently. Circle your tongue around the head, and then slide the head into your mouth. Create suction around the head . . .

—Dr. Judy Kuriansky

I'm kind of known for something that's not so great to be known for.

—Monica Lewinsky

You know the worst thing about oral sex? The view.

—Maureen Lipman

I wouldn't want the whole world to know how I do it . . . I had to spend three or four weeks learning how to keep from gagging, and how to breathe with the strokes.

—Linda Lovelace on her oral skills

I spent a great deal of time on my knees.

—Marilyn Monroe on casting directors

If you can't join 'em, lick 'em.

—Frederic Mullally on women

The professionals helped forge a common tongue. A man now had his joint copped, had some derby, or had his hat nailed to the ceiling. More frequently, men spoke of being blown or having a blow job (all since early twentieth c.).

—Lawrence Paros

Sex after children slows down. Every three months now we have sex. Every time I have sex, the next day I pay my quarterly taxes. Unless it's oral sex—then I renew my driver's license.

—Ray Romano

Beyond any doubt her sex is a mouth and a voracious mouth which devours the penis—a fact which can easily lead to the idea of castration. The amorous act is the castration of the man; but this is above all because sex is a hole.

—Jean-Paul Sartre

My mother gained a little bit of weight because she quit smoking. That's all right, but it's hard to listen to her reasoning. It's hard to have your mom tell you that she has an oral fixation and always has to have something in her mouth.

—David Spade

What's the big deal? President Clinton did it.

—Unidentified girl in middle school active in an "oral sex ring"

I would much rather have the children of the United States know about oral sex than listen to Oral Roberts.

—Gore Vidal

According to the polls, 12 percent of the American public thinks that oral sex isn't sex. I'll bet they just don't know how to do it correctly.

—Jimmy Williams

Some men know that a light touch of the tongue, running from a woman's toes to her ears, lingering in the softest way possible in various places in between, given often enough and sincerely enough, would add immeasurably to world peace.

—Marianne Williamson

It's amazing what you run into on the road. These chicks are ready for anything. They'll give head without thinking about it—anyplace: backstage, in the dressing room, out in the street. Anyplace, anytime.

—Frank Zappa on groupies

Orgasms

I may not be a great actress but I've become the greatest at screen orgasms. Ten seconds of heavy breathing, roll your head from side to side, simulate a slight asthma attack, and die a little.

—Candice Bergen

The residue of virility in the woman's orgasm is utilized by nature in order to eroticize her: otherwise the functioning of the maternal apparatus would wholly submerge her in the painful tasks of reproduction and motherhood.

—Marie Bonaparte

She will have to get her ecstasy of orgasm some other way. She will have to achieve that elsewhere—maybe with a vibrator.

—Ernie Chambers on a female
attorney general trying to get
a convicted killer executed

Premature ejaculation, I don't believe in that. If I come, it was right on time, that's the way I see it. As far as I'm concerned I can't come fast enough. They're mad at me because we have different goals in sex: I'm a speedfucker.

—Dave Chapelle

Come is coming of age.

—Cameron Diaz

When modern woman discovered the orgasm it was, combined with modern birth control, perhaps the biggest single nail in the coffin of male dominance.

—Eva Figes

Women fake orgasms if they really care about the man because they don't want him to feel a sense of failure . . . If they didn't fake it, and they learned how to relax, they would probably have their orgasm.

—Annie Flanders

As women have known since the dawn of our time, the primary site for stimulation to orgasm centers on the clitoris. The revolution unleashed by the Kinsey Report of 1953 has, by now, made this information available to men who, for whatever reason, had not figured it out for themselves by the more obvious routes of experience and sensitivity.

—Stephen Jay Gould

One orgasm in the bush is worth two in the hand.

—Graffito

So female orgasm is simply a nervous climax to sex relations . . . It may be thought of as a sort of pleasure prize that comes with a box of cereal. It is all to the good if the prize is there but the cereal is valuable and nourishing if it is not.

—Madeline Gray

When a pit bull romances your leg, fake an orgasm.
—Hut Landon

It happens to everybody. When it happens to me, I say, "Hey, you know, it's just my way of saying that I'm happy to see you."
—Richard Lewis on premature ejaculation

"Crime of passion"—that phrase drives me crazy. A man murdering his girlfriend is not a crime of passion. Premature ejaculation—that's a crime of passion.
—Hellura Lyle

Sex used to be our most powerful weapon against men. Not any more. Not since they found out we like it. We lost a big one there. Women aren't faking orgasms anymore. They're hiding them. "I didn't feel anything. Oh, that? That was the hiccups."
—Diane Nichols

What is an orgasm, after all, except laughter of the loins.
—Mickey Rooney

If you use the electric vibrator near water, you will come and go at the same time.
—Louise Sammons

The nature of female sexuality as here presented makes it clear that . . . Woman's inordinate orgasmic capacity did not evolve of monogamous, sedentary cultures.
—Mary Jane Sherfey

Living in New York is like coming all the time.
—Gene Simmons

The purpose of sex ideally is for the woman to attain orgasm and for the man not to.

—Sting

Women might be able to fake orgasms, but men can fake whole relationships.

—Sharon Stone

Hearing that there's no such thing as a vaginal orgasm was as good as news of the birth of Christ.

—Viva

An orgasm a day keeps the doctor away.

—Mae West

It is a fact terrible to contemplate, yet it is nevertheless true . . . That fully one-half of all women seldom or never experience any pleasure whatever in the sexual act. Now this is an impeachment of nature, a disgrace to our civilization.

—Victoria Claflin Woodhull

Orgies

Sex between a man and a woman can be wonderful—provided you get between the right man and the right woman.

—Woody Allen

If God had meant for us to have group sex, He'd have given us more organs.

—Malcolm Bradbury

I tried a five-way once, but I'm too needy. Afterward I was like, "So are we all in a relationship now?"
—Margaret Cho

At my age, I want two girls at once. If I fall asleep, they have each other to talk to.
—Rodney Dangerfield

Women are really not that exacting. They only desire one thing in bed. Take off your socks. And by the way— they're never going to invite their best girlfriend over for a threesome, so you can stop asking.
—Dennis Miller

An orgy looks particularly alluring seen through the mists of righteous indignation.
—Malcolm Muggeridge

I've never been in an orgy of more than three people.
—Jack Nicholson

You look for certain things in certain towns. Chicago, for instance, is notorious for sort of two things at once. Balling two chicks, or three, in combination acts.
—Jimmy Page

Once, a philosopher; twice, a pervert.
—Voltaire on being invited to an orgy for a second time.

Penis Envy

No woman except for so-called "deviants" seriously wishes to be male and have a penis. But most women would like to have the privileges and opportunities that go with it.

—Elena Gianini Belotti

I'm just a huge fan of the penis. Can I just say they're just the greatest? And they're all different—like snowflakes.

—Margaret Cho

Girls hold their mothers responsible for their lack of a penis and do not forgive her for their being thus put at a disadvantage.

—Sigmund Freud

The psychical consequences of penis envy are various and far reaching. After a woman has become aware of the wound to her narcissism, she develops, like a scar, a sense of inferiority. When she has passed beyond her first attempt at explaining her lack of a penis as being punishment personal to herself and has realized that sexual character is a universal one, she begins to share the contempt felt by men for a sex which is the lesser in so important a respect.

—Sigmund Freud

I wouldn't want a penis. It would be like a third leg. It would seem like a contraption that would get in your way.

—Madonna

Freud, or course, was wrong when he claimed that women suffer from penis envy—it is the men who do.

—Sabrina Sedgewick

My theory is that women don't suffer from penis envy. Every man just thinks his penis is enviable. Maybe Freud suffered from penis doubt.

—Bob Smith

I have enough trouble with what I have.

> —Sharon Stone on her gun
> ownership masking a Freudian
> penis envy

Philosophies

Love is so much better when you are not married.

> —Maria Callas

Sex ought to be a wholly satisfying link between two affectionate people from which they emerge unanxious, rewarded and ready for more.

> —Dr. Alex Comfort

Physiological expenditure is a superficial way of self expression. People who incline towards physical love accomplish nothing at all.

> —Salvador Dali

No sex is better than bad sex.

> —Germaine Greer

It is better to copulate than never.

> —Robert Heinlein

Love between the sexes is a sin in theology, a forbidden intercourse in jurisprudence, a mechanical insult in medicine, and a subject philosophy has no time for.

> —Karl Kraus

Who loves not wine, women and song
Remains a fool his whole life long.

> —Martin Luther

147

Pussy rules the world.

—Madonna

The other night I was making love to my wife, and she said, "deeper, deeper." So I started quoting Nietzsche to her.

—Dennis Miller

There are two things a real man likes—danger and play; and he likes woman because she is the most dangerous of playthings.

—Friedrich Nietzsche

Man should be trained for war and woman for the recreation of the warrior.

—Friedrich Nietzsche

I sport a cave-man mentality. A woman should be a lady on your arm and a whore behind your door.

—Nikki Sixx

I have always detested the belief that sex is the chief bond between man and woman. Friendship is far more human.

—Agnes Smedley

Sex is like money; only too much is enough.

—John Updike

Sex is conversation carried out by other means.

—Peter Ustinov

All discarded lovers should be given a second chance, but with somebody else.

—Mae West

Politics

The last important human activity not subject to taxation is sex.

—Russell Baker

Men in power always seem to get involved in sex scandals, but women don't even have a word for "male bimbo." Except maybe "senator."

—Elayne Boosler

But I want to say one thing to the American people. I want you to listen to me. I'm going to say this again. I did not have sexual relations with that woman, Miss Lewinsky. I never told anybody to lie, not a single time. Never. These allegations are false. And I need to go back to work for the American people.

—Bill Clinton

This is not about sex. This is not about lying about sex. It is, rather, when under oath does one lie about sex.

—George Gekas on Bill Clinton

Well, Teddy, I see you've changed your position on off-shore drilling.

—Howell Heflin on seeing a
photo of Ted Kennedy in a
compromising position with
a woman in a boat

You cannot decree women to be sexually free when they are not economically free.

—Shere Hite

I don't mind being regarded as perverted and unnatural, but I would die if people thought I was a Democrat.

—Florence King

I would rather have a president who does it to a woman than a president who does it to his country.

—Shirley MacLaine

If a man is running the country great and going out at night dressed as a woman, is it really our business?

—Paul Reiser

The only reason I'm not running for president is I'm afraid no woman would come forth and say she slept with me.

—Garry Shandling

I'm available to make love to Saddam Hussein to achieve peace in the Middle East.

—Ilona Staller

It was the first female-style revolution: no violence and we all went shopping.

—Gloria Steinem on the fall of
the Berlin Wall

Pornography

Mind and body are not to be taken lightly. Their connection is intimate and mysterious, and better mapped by poets than pornographers.

—Shana Alexander

When I was a kid I once stole a pornographic book in braille and rubbed the dirty parts.

—Woody Allen

Pornography exists for the lonesome, the ugly, the fearful . . . It's made for the losers.

—Rita Mae Brown

Pornography is the undiluted essence of anti-female propaganda.

—Susan Brownmiller

I happen to like old-school porn because I like the natural body. The women in this new porn, their boobs are just so weird and high and far out, they look like those goldfish with the puffy eyes.

—Margaret Cho

But many people in porn are more bourgeois than decadent, with boyfriends, husbands; they go to work. Bottom line, they're actors creating an illusion, like someone who plays a drunk or an addict.

—Brian De Palma

I think porn is fine. I like to watch people fuck.

—David Duchovny

Erotica is simply high-class pornography; better produced, better conceived, better executed, better packaged, designed for a better class of consumer.

—Andrea Dworkin

They are doing things on the screen these days that the French don't even put on postcards.

—Bob Hope

Everybody got it wrong. I said I was into porn again, not born again.

—Billy Idol

Okay, if you want to get down to the nitty gritty... Let's say I'm watching a porno, for instance—and I've analyzed it, to see what makes me tick—I do like to see two women together. It turns me on more than anything else. That's what rings my chimes.

—Tom Jones

For many feminists, pornography is the theory and rape is the practice.

—Chris Kramarae and
Paula A. Treichler

Pornography is literature designed to be read with one hand.

—Angela Lambert

Pornography is the attempt to insult sex, to do dirt on it.

—D. H. Lawrence

The difference between pornography and erotica is lighting.

—Gloria Leonard

Pornography is a direct denial of the power of the erotic, for it represents the suppression of true feeling. Pornography emphasizes sensation without feeling.

—Audre Lorde

I would like to see all people who read pornography or have anything to do with it put in a mental hospital for observation so we could find out what we have done to them.

—Linda Lovelace

Sick and perverted always appeals to me.

—Madonna

Obscenity is a cleansing process, whereas pornography only adds to the murk.

—Henry Miller

I'm someone who is on the record as being pro-pornography—all the way from kiddie porn and snuff films.

—Camille Paglia

Pornography is in the groin of the beholder.

—Charles Rembar

Experiences aren't pornographic; only images and representations—structures of the imagination—are.

—Susan Sontag

What pornographic literature does is precisely to drive a wedge between one's existence as a full human being and one's existence as sexual being—while in ordinary life a healthy person is one who prevents such a gap from opening up.

—Susan Sontag

If we define pornography as any message from any commercial medium that is intended to arouse sexual excitement, then it is clear that most advertisements are covertly pornographic.

—Philip Stater

Erotica is about sexuality, but pornography is about power and sex-as-a-weapon, in the same way we have come to understand that rape is about violence, and not really about sex at all.

—Gloria Steinem

Pornography is not about sex. It's about an imbalance of male-female power that allows and even requires sex to be used as a form of aggression . . . But until we finally untangle sexuality and aggression, there will be more pornography and less erotica. There will be little murders in our beds—and very little love.

—Gloria Steinem

The worst that can be said about pornography is that it leads not to anti-social acts but to the reading of more pornography.

—Gore Vidal

Press

I'd rather ride down the street on a camel than give . . . an in-depth interview. I'd rather ride down the street on a camel nude. In a snowstorm. Backward.

—Warren Beatty

I would like to take this opportunity to tell the press to kiss my skinny white ass.

—Calista Flockhart on
speculation she has an eating
disorder

They can wiggle their waggles in front of her face as far as I'm concerned.

—Victor Kiam on women
reporters in a pro football
locker room

I don't talk to people when I'm naked, especially women, unless they're on top of me or I'm on top of them.

—Jack Morris, baseball player, to
a female reporter in the locker
room

They are trying to prove their manhood.

—H. Ross Perot on female
reporters asking tough
questions

Hell hath no fury like a hooker with a press agent.

—Frank Sinatra on Judith
Campbell's claim that Sinatra
introduced her to John F.
Kennedy

Profanity

Fuck everybody.

—Cher

You can't keep people from telling dirty jokes. Fart jokes, ejaculation jokes—we're animals and we think they're funny.

—Michael Crichton

You won't find a single four-letter word in there. I don't go for that bullshit.

—Bob Feller on his
autobiography

The word "fuck" appears thirty times, the word "cunt" fourteen times, the word "balls" thirteen times, "shit" six times, "arse" and "piss" three times apiece.

—Mervyn Griffith-Jones on
Lady Chatterley's Lover

My mother never saw the irony in calling me a son-of-a-bitch.

—Jack Nicholson

The nowadays ruling that no word is unprintable has, I think, done nothing whatever for beautiful letters . . . Obscenity is too valuable a commodity to chuck around all over the place; it should be taken out of the safe on special occasions only.

—Dorothy Parker

Fuck is one of a group of well-known four letter words, all Anglo-Saxon, or Old English, in origin, that are uncomplicated, easy to pronounce, and monosyllabic.

—Alan Richter

It's hard to be funny when you have to be clean.

—Mae West

Professions/Careers

I cannot think of anything grimmer than being an aging actress—God! It's worse than being an aging homosexual.

—Candice Bergen

The term working mother is redundant.

—Erma Bombeck

Women dig [my act] because—I mean, you know this for a fact—women in private are much filthier than guys.

—Andrew Dice Clay

"G" means the hero gets the girl. "R" means the villain gets the girl. And "X" means everybody gets the girl.

—Kirk Douglas

People assume you slept your way to the top. Frankly, I couldn't sleep my way to the middle.

—Joni Evans

I wanted to be an actress and a scholar too. My first move was to get a "Rolling Stone" as a boyfriend. I slept with three, then decided that the singer was the best bet.

—Marianne Faithfull

Industrial relations are like sexual relations. It's better between two consenting parties.

—Vic Feather

Advertising is the most fun you can have with your clothes on.

—Jerry Della Femina

157

If women can sleep their way to the top, how come they aren't there?

—Ellen Goodman

Being a newspaper columnist is like being married to a nymphomaniac. It's great for the first two weeks.

—Lewis Grizzard

She okays all my scripts. In my marital contract it's written that I can't do any sex scenes.

—Dustin Hoffman

There are very few jobs that actually require a penis or vagina. All other jobs should be open to everybody.

—Florynce Kennedy

There are a lot of chicks who get laid by the director and still don't get the part.

—Claudia Linnear

I live for meetings with men in suits. I love them because I know they had a really boring week and I walk in there with my orange velvet leggings and drop popcorn in my cleavage and then fish it out and eat it. I like that. I know I'm entertaining them, and I know that they know.

—Madonna

You can fake chemistry between people. You can fake sex, love, explosions, special effects, horror. There is no delineation between a love scene and a breakfast scene. One doesn't require more of the actor than the other.

—John Malkovich

This business has been taken over by low-life sluts.

—Bette Midler on Roseanne Barr
and other female comedians

I never set out to be a businessman. I just wanted to have fun, fuck chicks, and do drugs.

—Ozzy Osbourne

Don't tell my mother I work in an advertising agency—she thinks I play piano in a whorehouse.

—Jacques Seguela

Performing wouldn't be so bad if everyone in the audience could come up on stage and I could kiss them beforehand. As it is, it's like making love without any preliminary kissing.

—Carly Simon

A male gynecologist is like an auto mechanic who has never owned a car.

—Carrie Snow

The definition of woman's work is shit work.

—Gloria Steinem

I figure, people who make movies have sex once a year, and people who make television have sex three times a week.

—Matt Stone

Why is it men are permitted to be obsessed about their work, but women are only permitted to be obsessed about men?

—Barbra Streisand

I don't think it will hurt my career if people know I'm happily married. I think it's much sexier to be in love with your wife.

—Patrick Swayze

When you go on the road, there's nothing to do but do drugs and fuck.

—Steven Tyler

I suspect that one of the reasons we create fiction is to make sex exciting.

—Gore Vidal

Fuck scenes are just hard work. You're naked in front of 90 people with a woman you hardly know.

—Bruce Willis

I can always find plenty of women to sleep with, but the kind of woman that is really hard for me to find is a typist who can read my writing.

—Thomas Wolfe

Most leading men can't be supportive of my work because they are too concerned about themselves. Or their penises.

—Sean Young

Promiscuity

Had nature formed me of the other sex, I should certainly have been a rover.

—Abigail Adams

We are on a sexual binge in this country . . . One consequence of this binge is that while people now get into bed more readily and a lot more naturally than they once did, what happens there often seems less important.

—Shana Alexander

There's another kind of promiscuity that I call environmental promiscuity. Here children grow up seeing casual sex all around them. They don't learn that there is any other way to behave sexually.

—Mary Calderone

Yes, that's correct—20,000 different ladies. At my age that equals out to having sex with 1.2 women everyday, everyday since I was fifteen.

—Wilt Chamberlain

Ooooh! Ahhh! Get out!

—Andrew Dice Clay on a one-night stand

In my youth I used to pick up sluts. I don't mean that nastily. It's a term of endearment.

—Kevin Costner

I can cat around a bit, but she can't.

—Eric Dickerson on his girlfriend

We were never friends. We just fucked.

—Boy George on bandmate Jon Moss

Virtually any man will sleep with any attractive young woman. In Washington the liberated princess can sleep with senators. In Hollywood, with directors and movie stars. Everywhere she can sleep with her boss.

—George Gilder

As a guy, you're raised to get as much as you can. Sex, sex, sex, that's what you're after. After a while, I realized what I was doing was foolhardy. Still, it took some time to travel from the brain groinward.

—Woody Harrelson

I have so much cybersex, my baby's first words will be, "You've got mail."

—Paulara R. Hawkins

Michael Jackson is the polar opposite of President Clinton. Michael Jackson is constantly, constantly, desperately trying to make us believe he's having sex with women.

—David Letterman

Easy is an adjective used to describe a woman who has the sexual morals of a man.

—Nancy Linn-Desmond

Promiscuous . . . A sordid word, reducing many valuable moments to nothing more than dog-like copulation.

—Marya Mannes

When I came into my hotel room last night, I found a strange blonde in my bed. I would stand for none of her nonsense! I gave her exactly twenty-four hours to get out.

—Groucho Marx

Boredom is often the cause of promiscuity, and always its result.

—Mignon McLaughlin

I'm always looking for meaningful one night stands.

—Dudley Moore

I'd wake up in the morning thinking, "I don't know your name, I don't know where you're from, and I know I'm not the first guy you've done this week."

—Ozzy Osbourne

I've noticed that as my reputation grows worse, my success with women increases.

—Roman Polanski

She knew, even though she was too young to know the reason, that indiscriminate desire and unselective sex were possible only to those who regarded sex and themselves as evil.

—Ayn Rand

I consider promiscuity immoral. Not because sex is evil, but because sex is too good and too important.

—Ayn Rand

I can't get enough women. I have sex as often as possible.

—Axl Rose

You cannot separate young limbs and lechery.

—William Shakespeare

I think it's natural for a man to be promiscuous . . . And you're talking to a guy who's just following his natural instincts.

—Gene Simmons

Women tend to think that because eggs are coming, they have to build a nest. Guys aren't like that. We roam, we plant our seeds and move on.

—Gene Simmons

Being with a woman all night never hurt no professional baseball player. It's staying up all night looking for a woman that does him in.

—Casey Stengel

You gotta learn that if you don't get it by midnight, chances are you ain't gonna get it; and if you do, it ain't worth it.

—Casey Stengel

Sex divorced from love is the thief of personal dignity.

—Caitlin Thomas

I started getting so screwed up that getting fucked up was more important than getting fucked. Part of me is still bummed out that I didn't have all the sex I could have had in the seventies.

—Steven Tyler

People called me the guy with the cock in his voice. Maybe that's why in eighty-four years of life I've been with over 145 women and girls.

—Rudy Vallee

The male equivalent of the nymphomaniac is Tom, Dick, Harry, and Joe, Pedro, Sam and every other red-blooded guy.

—Jimmy Williams

If I had done everybody I was supposed to have done just in this town [Hollywood], it [his penis] would have fallen off a long time ago.

—Henry Winkler

Prostitution

What's the difference between a whore and a congressman? A congressman makes more money.

—Edward Abbey

Too many cocks spoil the brothel.

—Polly Adler

The grocer, the butcher, the baker, the merchant, the landlord, the druggist, the liquor dealer. The policeman, the doctor, the city father and the politician—these are the people who make money out of prostitution.

—Polly Adler

Why is it immoral to be paid for an act that is perfectly legal if done for free?

—Gloria Allred and Lisa Bloom

A call girl is simply someone who hates poverty more than she hates sin.

—Sydney Biddle Barrows

On some level, almost every client wanted to believe that the girl was spending time with him not for money, but because she found him irresistible.

—Sydney Biddle Barrows

I am white and middle-class and ambitious, and I have no trouble identifying with either the call girl or the street hustler, and I can explain why in one sentence: I've been working to support myself in the city for fifteen years, and I've had more offers to sell my body for money than I have had to be an executive.

—Susan Brownmiller

165

A whore is a woman who takes more than she gives. A man who takes more than he gives is called a businessman.

—Charles Bukowski

Prostitution seems to be a problem. But what's the problem? Fucking is okay. Selling is okay. So why isn't selling fucking okay?

—George Carlin

Our hookers don't do it out of obligation, or necessity. Here, prostitution doesn't occur for that reason, but because, somehow, they like it.

—Fidel Castro

There are girls who manage to sell themselves, whom no one would take as a gift.

—Nicholas Chamfort

The archetypes of women are the Madonna and the whore. We're all like that, but we repress one side or the other.

—Laura Dern

A country without bordellos is like a house without bathrooms.

—Marlene Dietrich

You know, the biggest hooker in the world is a housewife. The only difference between a hooker and a housewife is the hooker does it with a lot of people. A wife only hooks for you, but she takes more money than a hooker would.

—Freddy Fender

I think I can truthfully say that my behavior in whore-houses has been exemplary.

—Errol Flynn

I may be good for nothing, but I'm never bad for nothing.

—Ginny

Whether our reformers admit it or not, the economic and social inferiority of women is responsible for prostitution.

—Emma Goldman

It was unbelievable to tell girls that being a prostitute after college while deciding on your career is okay because you'll meet your Prince Charming. It infuriated me.

—Daryl Hannah on the movie
Pretty Woman

Prostitution gives her an opportunity to meet people. It provides fresh air and wholesome exercise, and it keeps her out of trouble.

—Joseph Heller

My method is basically the same as Masters and Johnson, only they charge thousands of dollars and it's called therapy. I charge fifty dollars and it's called prostitution.

—Xavier Hollander

I've always maintained that there's a little bit of prostitute in all women. Or there should be. I think in order for a woman to be all that she hopes to be for a man, there has to be some of that there.

—Shirley Jones

It is better to have loved and lost than to have paid for it and not liked it.

—Hiram Kasten

If I still had a cherry, it would have been pushed back so far I could use it for a tail light.

—Nell Kimball

Prostitution may not be legal. But it sure is legitimate.

—Maggie

A reformed woman of the streets is the best of women.

—Mexican proverb

Women are the political prisoners of the feminist movement . . . They are considered criminals for no other reason than the fact they are women . . . Men aren't jailed for solicitation . . . Women are jailed. And they're jailed because they have cunts.

—Kate Millett

I though it was a pretty good deal. At the beach I was almost naked for nothing.

—Marilyn Monroe on getting paid for sex

Good taste and humor are a contradiction in terms, like a chaste whore.

—Malcolm Muggeridge

Prostitution testifies to the amoral power struggle of sex, which religion has never been able to stop. Prostitutes, pornographers, and their patrons are marauders in the forest of archaic night.

—Camille Paglia

Men need to be despunked regularly. It's when they're not getting regular despunking that they start causing problems. I call that a service, not a nuisance.

—Cynthia Payne

I'm sick and tired of everybody worrying about being politically correct. It's all bullshit. For instance, there are no more car thieves. They're nontraditional commuters. Homeless people are full-time outdoorsmen. Prostitutes are sexual maintenance partners.

—Paul Rodriguez

Hey, I didn't care if Dick called himself Napoleon, as long as his money was green.

—Sherry Rowland on Dick Morris telling her he was a presidential advisor

I think prostitutes are generally happy about being prostitutes. It's not a bad way to make a living.

—Ken Russell

Prostitution means sexual intercourse between a man and a woman aimed at satisfying the man's sexual and the woman's economic needs. It is obvious that sexual needs, even in a male dominated system, are not as urgent and important as economic needs which, if not satisfied, lead to disease and death. Yet society considers the woman's economic need as less vital than the man's sexual one.

—Nawal El Saadawi

I did not find the business all that disgusting. You pick your customers, you meet interesting people and youth is not a prerequisite.

—Margo St. James

Better an old maid than a young whore.
—Scottish proverb

It is a silly question to ask a prostitute why she does it . . . These are the highest paid "professional" women in America.
—Gail Sheehy

The one thing prostitution is not is a "victimless crime." It attracts a wide species of preying criminals and generates a long line of victims, beginning with the most obvious and least understood—the prostitute herself.
—Gail Sheehy

It started to add up.
—Charlie Sheen admitting paying
$53,000 for call girls

Well, there's a book that says we're all sinners and I at least chose a sin that's made quite a few people happier than they were before they met me.
—Sally Stanford

Prostitutes believe in marriage. It provides them with most of their trade.
—Suzie

They're whores, and that's not a term of abuse. It's a good, honest, biblical word for an honorable profession of ancient lineage. They make love with men for a living and don't you ever think badly of them for that. Any woman worthy of the name would do the same if her children were hungry.
—Allegra Taylor

So-called decent women differ from whores mainly in that whores are less dishonest.
—Leo Tolstoy

The most interesting woman characters in a picture are whores, and every man in love is a sex pervert at heart.
—Billy Wilder

She was so exquisite a whore
That in the belly of her mother
Her cunt was placed so right before
Her father fucked them both together.
—John Wilmot

A hooker told me she'd do anything I wanted for fifty bucks. I said, "Paint my house."
—Henny Youngman

Religion

The pope is a hard guy to please, isn't he? No weird sex. Well, what's this kiss my ring stuff?
—Elayne Boosler

I don't want to control anybody's mind or anybody's heart—I just want to help free people from the concept of sex as evil instead of a gift from God.
—Mary Calderone

Who do atheists talk to during sex?
—Karen Chatelle

It brought me closer to God.
—Jessica Hahn on posing nude for *Playboy*

Such behavior is not just inappropriate—it is immoral.

> —Joseph Lieberman on
> Bill Clinton's conduct with
> Monica Lewinsky

I was wondering today what the religion of the country is, and all I could come up with is sex.

> —Clare Boothe Luce

Nuns are sexy.

> —Madonna

In some remote regions of Islam it is said a woman caught unveiled by a stranger will raise her skirt to cover her face.

> —Raymond Mortimer

Sex had become the religion of the most civilized portions of the earth. The orgasm has replaced the Cross as the focus of longing and the image of fulfillment.

> —Malcolm Muggeridge

If you offered me a passionate love affair and you offered me a high priestess role in a fabulous castle above a cliff where I can just, like, live a very spiritual kind of religious-library-communing-with-the-stars, learning kind of existence, I'm going to go for the high priestess.

> —Stevie Nicks

I've been a man many times. That's what I'm trying to atone for now.

> —Helen Reddy on reincarnation

Men reach their sexual peak at eighteen. Women reach theirs at thirty-five. Do you get the feeling that God is playing a practical joke?

—Rita Rudner

As the French say, "There are three sexes—men, women and clergymen."

—Rev. Sydney Smith

Religion is probably, after sex, the second oldest resource which human beings have available to them for blowing their minds.

—Susan Sontag

In an age in which greed and lust stalk the land like some Biblical plague, it is easy to view sex as just one more thing to be had. It is the mythos of moderns.

—Jennifer Stone

If you're only going to have ten rules, I don't know if adultery should be one of them.

—Ted Turner on revising the Ten Commandments

Christ kept me from touching women for a long time, and when I did fall a little, I never fell completely. Even in our marriage, Miss Vicki and I never have S-E-X unless it's to have children.

—Tiny Tim

God created sex. Priests created marriage.

—Voltaire

Sex and religion are bordering states. They use the same vocabulary, share like ecstasies, and often serve as a substitute for one another.

—Jessamyn West

See, the problem is that God gives men a brain and a penis, and only enough blood to run one at a time.

—Robin Williams

Seduction

[He] twisted my nipples as though tuning a radio.

—Lisa Alther

Hello, gorgeous. Could we discuss the possibility of rape?

—Joan Baez to Don Johnson

All a writer has to do to get a woman is to say he's a writer. It's an aphrodisiac.

—Saul Bellow

I tell women that the face is my experience and the hands are my soul—anything to get those panties down.

—Charles Bukowski

I'm not good in bed. Hell, I'm not even good on the couch.

—Drew Carey

George Moore unexpectedly pinched my behind. I felt rather honored that my behind should have drawn the attention of the great master of English prose.

—Ilka Chase

The seduction emanating from a person of uncertain or dissimulated sex is powerful.

—Colette

How a man must hug, and dandle, and kittle, and play a hundred little tricks with his bedfellow when he is disposed to make that use of her that nature designed for her.

—Erasmus

It's marvelous being a seductress.

—Mia Farrow on stealing André
Previn away from his wife

She thinks there is a close correlation between the men she can seduce and the men she might marry. But a young princess can seduce the vast majority of men. Unless very securely married.

—George Gilder

The 1950s were ten years of foreplay.

—Germaine Greer

Men are brought up to command, women to seduce.

—Sally Kempton

Have you seen a copy of *Tax Tips for Billionaires?*

—David Letterman on pick-up
lines in a bookstore

Kissing, fondling and foreplay are regarded as the height of bad behavior among the tribe and its culture contains not one romantic song or story. There is no Manuan word for love.

—Margaret Mead on the Manus
tribe of the Admiralty Islands

If you see a man playing with his penis in front of you, you don't think it's a cop.

—George Michael on the cop
that busted him

A girl whose cheeks are covered with paint
has an advantage with me over one whose ain't.

—Ogden Nash

What they [girls] love to yield they would often rather have stolen. Rough seduction delights them, the boldness of near rape is a compliment.

—Ovid

Men seldom make passes
at girls who wear glasses.

—Dorothy Parker

To attract men I wear a perfume called "New Car Interior."

—Rita Rudner

You can seduce a man's wife . . . attack his daughter, and wipe your hands on his canary, but if you don't like his movie, you're dead.

—Joseph von Sternberg

A fox is a wolf who sends flowers.

—Ruth Weston

Sex Appeal

I was what's called rather unhandsomely, "highly sexed." But it was such a surprise that one could attract.

—Enid Bagnold

A good actress lasts, sex attraction does not.
—Brigitte Bardot

I don't look any better than I did ten years ago. How come all these girls are coming on to me now? Where were they in high school when I needed them?
—Billy Joel

Men aren't attracted to me by my mind. They're attracted by what I don't mind.
—Gypsy Rose Lee

I think my own desire to be loved is what makes me sexually attractive.
—Dudley Moore

I have so little sex appeal that my gynecologist calls me sir.
—Joan Rivers

This sex attraction, though it is useful for keeping the world peopled, has nothing to do with beauty: it blinds us to ugliness instead of opening our eyes to beauty.
—George Bernard Shaw

If a man doesn't look at me when I walk into a room, he's gay.
—Kathleen Turner

The label sex goddess somehow eclipses everything else about you . . . She has no intellect, no emotions, no anything.
—Raquel Welch

Sexual Knowledge

I was incredible last night in bed. I never once had to sit up and consult the manual.

—Woody Allen

I am constantly amazed when I talk to young people to learn how much they know about sex and how little about soap.

—Billie Burke

At least some of the men who write sex books admit they really don't understand female sexuality. Freud was one. Masters is another—that was why he got Johnson.

—Arlene Croce

If you bring a plastic penis into the classroom as they do in Sweden, that removes all the mystery.

—Jane Fonda

If I were asked for a one-line answer to the question, "What makes a woman good in bed?" I would say, "A man who is good in bed."

—Bob Guccione

Good lovers have known for centuries that the hand is probably the primary sex organ.

—Eleanor Hamilton

All too many men still seem to believe, in a rather naive and egocentric way, that what feels good to them is automatically what feels good to a woman.

—Shere Hite

Children are satisfied with the stork story up to a certain age because the little fartlings are the world's most crustaceous reactionaries; they don't want to know, they don't want their preconceived opinions toppled.

—Florence King

The female sex drive is sixty percent vanity, thirty percent curiosity, and ten percent physical.

—Florence King

There is nothing that impairs a man's sexual performance quicker than any suggestion that he's not doing it right.

—Helen Lawrenson

If I ever wrote a sex manual, it would be called, *Ouch, You're on My Hair.*

—Richard Lewis

I actually learned about sex watching neighborhood dogs . . . I think the most important thing I learned was: never let go of the girl's leg no matter how hard she tries to shake you off.

—Steve Martin

The best sex education for kids is when daddy pats mommy on the fanny when he comes home from work.

—William Masters

Lets teach a . . . follow-up class to sex education. Call it reality 101—hammering home to a sixteen-year-old teen that he or she is going to have to quit school, quit video games, quit hanging out, and work a fifty-hour week dumping frozen chicken tenders into hot oil just so you can keep little Scooter Junior in Similac. Trust me, that's a bigger deterrent to teenage sex than the backseat of a Yugo.

—Dennis Miller

It is far easier to explain to a three-year-old how babies are made than to explain the process whereby bread or sugar appear on the table.

—Dervla Murphy

Women should restrain provocative behavior, [so men can] work on other than genital forms of personal communications.

—Polish Education Ministry sex
education guide

In sexual intercourse it's quality not quantity that counts.

—Dr. David Reubin

Sex is something I really don't understand too hot. You never know where the hell you are. I keep making up these sex rules for myself, and then I break them right away.

—J. D. Salinger

Sexuality education is a lifelong process of acquiring information and forming attitudes, beliefs and values about identity, relationships and intimacy. It encompasses sexual development, reproductive health, interpersonal relationships, affection, intimacy, body image and gender roles.

—Sexual Information and
Education Council of the
United States

By the time he finishes defining sex, I think I'll learn that I'm actually a virgin.

—Scarlet Thomas on Bill Clinton's definitions

Sexually Transmitted Diseases

Every time you sleep with a boy you sleep with all his old girlfriends.

—AIDS advertisement, 1987

Wouldn't it be great if we found you could only get AIDS from giving money to TV preachers?

—Elayne Boosler

Take the wife.

—Edwina Currie on how to avoid catching AIDS when traveling

We practice safe sex. We gave up the chandelier a long time ago.

—Kathie Lee Gifford

Life is a sexually transmitted disease.

—Graffito

Remember when safe sex meant your parents had gone away for the weekend?

—Rhonda Hansome

Safe sex is very important. That's why I'm never doing it on a plywood scaffolding again.

—Jenny Jones

For the first time in history, sex is more dangerous than the cigarette afterwards.

—Jay Leno

When they said "Make love not war" at Woodstock, they never imagined that one would become as dangerous as the other.

—Jay Leno

I went on a date. I said, "I like you, but can we just boil ourselves before we get into bed."

—Richard Lewis

I tried phone sex and it gave me an ear infection.

—Richard Lewis

Nobody ever got cancer from sex.

—Marilyn Monroe

The only time I caught a venereal disease was from a Miss New York . . . I caught gonorrhea from Miss New York. Never got it from a Mexican whore.

—Nick Nolte

I have said it again and again. "Everyone who preached free love in the sixties is responsible for AIDS." And we must accept moral responsibility for it. The idea that it is an accident, a historical accident, a microbe that sort of fell from the heavens—absurd. We must face what we did.

—Camille Paglia

AIDS obliges people to think of sex as having, possibly, the direst consequences. Suicide; or murder.

—Susan Sontag

Who would have ever thought you could die from sex?
It was much more fun when you only went to hell.
—John Waters

Virtue

A pessimist is a man who thinks all women are bad; an
optimist is one who hopes they are.
—Chauncey M. Depew

Sexual morality, as society defines it, is contemptible.
—Sigmund Freud

Everything that used to be a sin is now a disease.
—Bill Maher

A bachelor's virtue depends upon his alertness; a married man's depends upon his wife's.
—H. L. Mencken

I have my standards. They may be low, but I have them.
—Bette Midler

Woman's virtue is a man's greatest invention.
—Cornelia Otis Skinner

When the sun comes up, I have morals again.
—Elizabeth Taylor

Be virtuous and you will be eccentric.
—Mark Twain

Virtue has its own reward, but it has no sale at the box
office.
—Mae West

You may have noted the fact that it is a person's virtue as often as his vices that make him difficult to live with.

—Kate Douglas Wiggins

Women represent the triumph of matter over mind: men represent the triumph of mind over morals.

—Oscar Wilde

Voyeurism/Exhibitionism

I like to be naked in movies. I have a reputation to up-hold.

—Alec Baldwin

I suppose the show wasn't going too well, so Jim decided to pull out his prick and liven it up a bit.

—John Lennon

I called my book *Sex* because it was a very provocative title and I knew people would want to buy it and look at the pictures and yet they denounce it at the same time, so I thought, that's a statement of our society in itself.

—Madonna

I would pay a guy who had a big penis to come and have sex with these ladies so I could watch them.

—Little Richard

It is better to be looked over than overlooked.

—Mae West

Women

For women the best aphrodisiacs are words. The G-Spot is in the ears. He who looks for it below is wasting his time.

—Isabel Allende

Every woman needs a man to discover her.

—Charlie Chaplin

Women want men, career, money, children, friends, luxury, comfort, independence, freedom, respect, love and a three dollar panty hose that won't run.

—Phyllis Diller

Why can't a woman be more like a dog? So sweet, loving, attentive.

—Kirk Douglas

There is no worse evil than a bad woman; and nothing has ever been produced better than a good one.

—Euripides

She that paints her face, thinks of her tail.

—Benjamin Franklin

Sex hasn't been the same since women started enjoying it.

—Lewis Grizzard

Nature has given women so much power that the law has very wisely given them little.

—Samuel Johnson

Attached to a woman's cunt was always the woman herself . . . The cunt was important sure, but that wasn't
the whole of it.

—Henry Miller

A smart girl is one who knows how to play tennis, piano
and dumb.

—Lynn Redgrave

Women are a lot like umpires. They make quick deci-
sions, never reverse them, and they don't think you're
safe when you're out.

—Pete Rose

The perfect woman has a brilliant brain, wants to make
love until four in the morning—and then turns into a
pizza.

—David Lee Roth

Women speak two languages—one of which is verbal.

—William Shakespeare

Women have a special corner of their hearts for sins
they have never committed.

—Cornelia Otis Skinner

Once a woman has given you her heart, you can never
get rid of the rest of her.

—John Vanbrugh

Women begin by resisting a man's advances and end by
blocking his retreat.

—Oscar Wilde

Women's Liberation

Men of sense in all ages abhor those customs which treat us only as the vassals of your sex.

—Abigail Adams

I don't know if women want all this equality. They're all different. A lot of women change their minds every twenty minutes.

—Tony Bennett

Feminists still don't acknowledge that the person who is sexually harassed has an enormous amount of power. Monica Lewinsky, for example, has shown she has quite a bit of power, hasn't she?

—Michael Crichton

Women's liberation calls it enslavement but the real truth about the sexual revolution is that it has made sex an almost chaotically limitless and therefore unmanageable realm in the life of a woman.

—Midge Decter

I'm really tired of feminists, sick of them. They've really dug themselves into their own grave. Any man would be a fool who didn't agree with equal rights and pay, but some women now, juggling with career, lover, children, wifehood, have spread themselves too thin and are very unhappy.

—Michael Douglas

Intercourse is the pure, sterile, formal expression of men's contempt for women.

—Andrea Dworkin

The major concrete achievement of the woman's movement of the 1970s was the "dutch treat."
—Nora Ephron

In a way, I think women's liberation is bullshit, but maybe it was necessary. A woman doing the same job as a man should be paid the same wage, but that's as far as I go.
—Peter Frampton

I get kicked around for saying it, but men and women are not equal . . . Feminists don't like me and I don't like them.
—Mel Gibson

True emancipation . . . will have to do away with the absurd notion of the dualism of the sexes, or that man and woman represent two antagonistic worlds.
—Emma Goldman

Men have always got so many "good reasons" for keeping their privileges. If we had left it to the men toilets would have been the greatest obstacle to human progress. Toilets were always the reason women couldn't become engineers, or pilots, or even members of parliament. They didn't have women's toilets.
—Hazel Hunkins Hallinan

The only alliance I would make with the woman's liberation movement is in bed.
—Abbie Hoffman

Women are the only exploited group in history to have been idealized into powerlessness.
—Erica Jong

I can't change my sex. But you can change your policy.
—Helen Kirkpatrick

Women's libbers are a pain in the ass. I treat women the way I always did, except I treat women's libbers different: if I catch one, I try and screw her a little harder.
—Evil Knievel

Feminism was established to allow unattractive women access to mainstream society.
—Rush Limbaugh

All these femi-nazis out there, demanding their right to abortion as the most important thing in their life never have to worry about having one anyway. Because who'd want to have sex with them.
—Rush Limbaugh

No one is going to take women's liberation seriously until women recognize that they will not be thought of as equals in the secret privacy of the men's most private mental part until they eschew alimony.
—Norman Mailer

I'm doing my bit for the woman's movement. Women have always been naked in movies, and now I'm just desperate to take my clothes off as much as possible.
—Ewan McGregor on nude
scenes

Every time we liberate a woman, we liberate a man.
—Margaret Mead

Women's liberation is just a lot of foolishness. It's men who are discriminated against. They can't bear children. And no one's likely to do anything about that.
—Golda Meir

My real attitude toward women is this, and it hasn't changed because of any movement or anything: basically, women like to be treated as sex objects.
—Roger Moore

Feminism is the result of a few ignorant and literal-minded women letting the cat out of the bag about which is the superior sex.
—P. J. O'Rourke

Feminism has crippled men. They don't know when to make a pass. If they do make a pass, they don't know if they're going to end up in court.
—Camille Paglia

Leaving sex to the feminists is like letting your dog vacation at the taxidermist.
—Camille Paglia

To demand equality between [a woman and a man] in any dirty work that stains her beauty and detracts from her femininity is unjust and cruel.
—Muammar al-Qaddafi

Even more than the pill, what has liberated women is that they no longer need to depend on men economically.
—Jane Bryant Quinn

Women's chains have been forged by men, not by anatomy.
—Estelle Ramey

To me, the important task of modern feminism is to accept and proclaim sex: to bury forever the lie that the body is a hindrance to the mind, and sex is a necessary evil to be endured for the perpetuation of our race.
—Dora Russell

Legislation and case law still exist in some parts of the United States permitting the "passion shooting of a wife"; the reverse, of course, is known as homicide.
—Diane B. Schulder

Women's discontent increases in exact proportion to her development.
—Elizabeth Cady Stanton

If women want any rights more than they have, why don't they just take them, and not be talking about it.
—Sojourner Truth

People call me a feminist whenever I express sentiments that differentiate me from a doormat or a prostitute.
—Rebecca West

I feel very empathetic [toward] women who are asked to wear low-cut things. I've never had to act in a film where they said, "Here, stuff this down your pants." I think it's hideous, what women are asked to do and what they're asked to stand for in films.
—Bruce Willis

Sexiness is no longer defined just as whether women are desirable, but also as what women desire. The more liberated women become—economically, politically, and personally—the more erotic we are. Freedom is a lot sexier than dependency.
—Naomi Wolf

Index of Sources